THE SIXTIES

D1232343

BIG IDEAS

General editor: Lisa Appignanesi

As the twenty-first century moves through its tumultuous first decade, we need to think about our world afresh. It's time to revisit not only politics, but our passions and preoccupations, and our ways of seeing the world. The Big Ideas series challenges people who think about these subjects to think in public, where soundbites and polemics too often provide sound and fury but little light. These books stir debate and will continue to be important reading for years to come.

Other titles in the series include:

Julian Baggini   **Complaint**
Paul Ginsborg   **Democracy**
Ian Hacking   **Identity**
Eva Hoffman   **Critical Time**
Steven Lukes   **Moral Relativism**
Susie Orbach   **Bodies**
Renata Salecl   **Tyranny of Choice**
Slavoj Žižek   **Violence**

THE SIXTIES

Jenny Diski

PROFILE BOOKS

First published in Great Britain in 2009 by
PROFILE BOOKS LTD
3A Exmouth House
Pine Street
London EC1R 0JH
www.profilebooks.com

1 3 5 7 9 10 8 6 4 2

Typeset in Minion by MacGuru Ltd
info@macguru.org.uk

Printed and bound in Great Britain by
Bell & Bain Ltd, Glasgow

A CIP catalogue record for this book is available from the
British Library.

ISBN 978 1 84668 003 8

For Roger with love

CONTENTS

Introduction   1

1
Consuming the Sixties   11

2
Altering Realities   31

3
Body Work   49

4
Remaking the World   69

5
Projecting the Future   97

6
Changing Our Minds   119

Notes   141
Index   145

INTRODUCTION

Now that it has gone, the twentieth century has become an idea. The past is always an idea which people have about it after the event. Those whose job it is to tell the story of the past in their own present call it history. To generations born later, receiving the recollections of their parents or grandparents, or reading the historians, the past is a story, a myth handily packaged into an era, bounded by a particular event – a war, a financial crisis, a reign, a decade, a century – anything that conveniently breaks the ongoing tick of time into a manageable narrative. Those people who were alive during the period in question, looking back, call it memory – memory being just another instance of the many ways in which we make stories. But although the past always belongs to the present and future, the later third of the twentieth century we know as the Sixties was one of those particular periods that was an idea to many even before it became the past. The Sixties were an idea in the minds, perhaps even more powerful than the experience, of those who were actually living though them.

As a rule, life has a quotidian way about it. Later, we tell ourselves we made decisions, thought this or that, came to a conclusion, but in each actual present moment we generally just react, and only afterwards name our reaction decision or thought, and designate it a place in what we like to think of as the continuum of our opinions, or belief or personality. It still feels to me as if life is an ongoing series of discrete moments, like the breaths we take, however much we want to solidify time, after the event, into something more consequential. Nevertheless, those of us who lived through the Sixties were as beguiled by our present then, as we are now that it is our past. It's not at all clear *whose* idea the Sixties was: but I suspect, as I repeatedly suggest in the following pages, that our parents, the generation whose youth was cut short by the Second World War and who so complained about their wild children's doings, had more to do with dreaming up and even sustaining the Sixties than we think. At any rate, the idea of the Sixties was pretty well in place by the time I got there in my mid-adolescence, and the concept strengthened as we lived it, moment by moment, and then told it in increasingly large episodes, played its music, moved through quite other present times, defended it (even while we sometimes mocked it) and passed the whole securely wrapped parcel on to new generations as the ideal of a time when it was really something to be young.

Looked at through our eyes – the baby boomers born immediately around and after the end of the war – things certainly have changed a good deal since the Sixties. Where we took mind-altering drugs to change our consciousness and find other ways of thinking about how to live, today the young take Es in order to dance longer without tiring, binge-drink until they fall over in the street, or snort cocaine in order to keep life a party.

Where we dropped out of university, fought against any establishment we could find and travelled the world to encounter different traditions of living, the present generation take a gap year to pop into the developing world before getting on with training for degrees to boost their income potential. Where we explored sexual freedom and began to think about the political nature of gender roles, the young clamour to be on *Big Brother* and have sex casually on TV in order to become fatuously famous...Unless, of course, that is as simplistic and establishment a view of the present world as we believed our parents' views of us to be. In truth, the only thing that is absolutely certain is that the music then was better.

The Sixties, of course, were not the decade of the same name. They began in the mid-1960s with the rise of popular culture (not with the Beatles, as Larkin said, nor with fucking, which had started even before the Stones were young), aided by a generation of people who did not have an urgent economic fear, nor (in Britain) a war to deal with, and it ended in the mid-1970s when all the open-ended possibilities we saw began to narrow, as disillusion, right-wing politicians, and the rest of our lives started to loom unexpectedly large. In his novel *Kensington Gardens*, Rodrigo Fresàn[1] suggests that the Sixties generation were the first fully to understand and try to live out Peter Pan's imperative never to grow up. We kept telling ourselves and each other that we were young, but now I think we had no idea what that meant (either that or I have no idea now) – because we had no notion, even if we vaguely knew we had to grow old, of ever not being young. Perhaps it was simply that a fortunate set of political and economic circumstances gave us the longest gap year in history. Perhaps the alternative ways of thinking and living were little more than an extended rave. And perhaps in the end we wearied of all that dispiriting casual sex, the trips to the STD clinic and the communal rows about who was going to do the washing-up and pay the gas bill, and began to like the idea of bourgeois homes, families and jobs. Who filled the planet with noxious gases and tore a hole in the ozone layer, who presided over a grasping globalisation that our children have taken to the streets to protest against? The music, however, was undeniably as great as we thought it was.

The Fifties, that long gasp after the end of the war, when so much had been damaged and so little had been mended, did not expire until the Sixties were well on in years. The generation that had won the war for us owned the world they had fought for and expected their children to take full advantage of the peace and plenty that was, surely, just around the corner. They suffered the war, they suffered the post-war austerity while making sure that we had the eggs and most of the meat rations. We were ready-made to fulfil a dream that seems to afflict parents in all times and places, that their children should be materially successful and therefore, by definition, happy. So it wasn't until the tough times had turned the corner and we were old enough to spit out the food they set aside for us, to scorn the careers they had to interrupt so that we could have better ones, to refuse to take advantage of the nicely made world they had arranged for us, that you could say the Sixties really started. We looked at the apparent calm, at the possibility of an untroubled suburban life that trickled properly and uneventfully to the grave, and didn't like what we saw at all. The higher education our parents were so proud to have achieved for some of us gave us time to wonder why we had to recreate the desired world of our parents. And those who did not go to university wondered why they had to spend their lives in factories replicating the passive acceptance of the status quo. It wasn't at all obvious to many of us, of many classes, why we had to go on going on. The Sixties when they finally came to each of us were a time of striving for individuality and a nagging urge to rebel against the dead middle of the twentieth century. Two generations before us had been involved in war. You need to go back to the young of the Twenties to find any similarity to the Sixties generation in the desire to hang on to irresponsibility, or childhood, whatever you want to call it; and to the young of the Thirties to find a serious attempt to take on an alternative politics. It may be that in the end, or from a present-day perspective, we were more like the generation of the Twenties.

But there was also the Cold War. The peaceful world our parents kept saying they had bequeathed to us was daily on the verge of exploding into the worst and final conflict. We expected it to happen. We considered what we would do with the four minutes that the early warning system promised us when a nuclear weapon was heading our way. The 'everything is all right now' our parents told us about was always being undercut by the doctrine of Mutually Assured Destruction. An ever-darkening mushroom cloud loomed over the endlessly blue horizon.

The argument we had with our parents was the initial key to the Sixties, but perhaps (because in Britain we had no national catastrophe to battle against and the Cold War was entirely out of our control) we were the first youth cohort to feel free enough from guilt and obligation to repudiate the old ways. Of course, we acted in the shadow of the Beats and Existentialists of the previous decade, and the distinction between them and us in terms of opposition was slighter than we imagined. It may be that even the distinction between us and our parents was slighter than we imagined. Quite without irony, in walking away from the domestic and cultural structures of the Fifties and before, we found and formed our own quite rigid self-affirming groups in order to demand the right to express our individuality. Though all reactionaries were reactionary in much the same way, there were many ways to be radical in the Sixties. But, unsurprisingly, they were often mutually exclusive. We recreated the old divisions in what only seemed to be new forms. It was just a matter of time (and our later readings of Foucault) before it turned out (to our unacknowledged relief, perhaps?) that the over-arching structures had been built to survive our (or any) assault on them, and the world remained unrocked – except, of course, let us never forget, by the music.

The early years of the twenty-first century are the right time to look at the idea that was the Sixties, and to examine the intentions and legacy of the generation that lived it, because we are old enough now to see where we went in relation to where we thought we were going. The Sixties people are in their sixties. It has been more than forty years since the world was ours for the taking and shaping. We can look back with nostalgia to the simple fact of being young or we can try and tease out what, actually, we were up to and why; whether the influences on us and our own ideas were as new as they seemed, and whether we were as serious as we thought we were about changing the world. And to what extent there was any reality to the idea we once had and to the idea our children have received, of that time when we were young.

What follows is a personal memoir to a very large extent – and after all, weren't the Sixties accused above all of having consolidated the sense of the self which created that most monstrous beast: the Me Generation? I'm qualified only to speak about the Sixties then and now as I lived them then and now. I lived in London during that period, regretting the Beats, buying clothes, going to movies, dropping out, reading, taking drugs, spending time in mental hospitals, demonstrating, having sex, teaching. America was very far away. My first visit was in 1974 (where I place the end of the Sixties), and there was a powerful sense of aftermath by the time I arrived as the Watergate hearings were coming to an end. But what happened there, in the Sixties, mattered very much, as the news arrived, or the drugs or the songs. I listened very carefully to the messages from across the ocean. I couldn't begin to live the reality of the Vietnam war or the civil rights movement, but they rippled though my daily life and thought. America was a backcloth, a colour wash in my Sixties, its ever-presence was how I enlarged the small world of London and the slightly larger world of Europe, and how I developed my sense of who I was and where in the world I belonged. Nevertheless, being in London was very particular.

What the American and British baby boomers, who inhabited the Sixties as if they were building a new planet, have in common is that we watched the radicalism we thought we understood and embodied turn into a radicalism we (ignorantly and naively) never dreamed of. Perhaps all the hope and disappointment hung on a simple definition of a word or two. The big idea we had – though heaven knows it wasn't new – was freedom, liberty, permission, a great enlarging of human possibilities beyond the old politenesses and restrictions. But it was an idea we failed to think through. It was a failure of thought essentially, rather than a failure of imagination. We were completely wrong-footed when the Sixties turned inexorably into the Eighties. With Margaret Thatcher and Ronald Reagan presiding, our favourite words – freedom, liberty, permission – were bandied about anew and dressed in clothes that made them unrecognisable to us. But even back then, in the Sixties, while we used the word 'liberty' there were others who also used it, sometimes varying it to 'libertarian', who meant something quite different from what we intended, and we nodded and smiled, taking them to our bosom, and completely failing to understand that they meant a world that was diametrically opposed to the one we intended to inhabit.

We really didn't see it coming, the new world of rabid individualism and the sanctity of profit. But perhaps that is only to be expected. It's possible after all that we were simply young, and now we are simply old and looking back as every generation does nostalgically to our best of times. Perhaps the Sixties are an idea that has had its day and lingers long after its time. Except, of course, for the music.

1

CONSUMING THE SIXTIES

Making money is art, and working is art and good business is the best art.

The Philosophy of Andy Warhol, 1975

It was a black crêpe dress, implacably black was how I thought of it, cut like a skating dress, long-waisted, with a very short skirt. It zipped from the small of the back to a high close-fitting turtle-neck that matched the tubelike, skin-tight long black sleeves. The bodice outlined my small breasts and skimmed my torso, continuing smoothly down to my jutting hipbones from where the dropped waist attached to a skirt that flared out very gently, just enough to fall loosely to the hem. It was completely unadorned, no decoration, nothing to alleviate the dense, unreflective blackness. It might have been a dress for mourning in, the most severe imaginable, except for the way it silhouetted my body and the fact that it stopped ten inches and more above my knees. My legs were covered in sheer cobweb-grey tights and I wore a pair of chisel-toed black patent flat shoes with a sharply squared brass buckle on the front. The buckle was the only colour or detail I wore apart from several geometric silver rings on my fingers. My long hair was pulled tightly back and twisted into the nape of my neck, like a ballerina. I wore my usual make-up: deathly pale foundation, white lipstick, white eyeshadow, my lids thickly outlined in painted black, with several layers of mascara emphasising my upper and lower lashes. Under my lower eyelids I had painted extra fine, vertical black lines, sunray style. I, like my dress, looked implacable.

When I checked myself in the mirror before going out, what I saw was the reincarnation of a girl I had spoken to once when I was a child at the skating rink my mother took me to every day. The girl and I practised spins and figures in the more or less empty centre, while less constrained skaters whizzed round and round us at the edges of the rink. She was at least fourteen or fifteen, and I was just six or seven. To me, she was a goddess, skating like a champion, spinning on the spot, her head dropped back looking up at her fingertips just touching each other to form an arch over herself. She was the most perfect age I could imagine, and all the more worthy of worship because she was dressed incomprehensibly from head to foot in black – her hair-enclosing snood, short dress, thick tights, skating boots and gloves were all relentlessly black. It was a colour only old ladies wore in those days. I finally got up courage to ask her at the end of one of her spins why she was all in black. She looked down at me for a moment with a wonderfully melancholic expression, and told me solemn-faced, 'I am in mourning for my life.' I was far too young to recognise the adolescent melodrama of her dress or the existentially induced world-weary self-description. She was the most magnificent, most mysteriously glamorous creature I had ever seen.

My version of her dress fourteen years on had come from Biba in Kensington Church Street. Swirly art deco, black and gold interior, dim lights, loud psychedelic pop music, feather boas, wild hats, floaty garments for drifting around in at home or at parties, slick mini-dresses to snap about the streets in, everything hung from wooden coatstands – oh, and another memorable treasure on which I spent all my money one week: a silver and black striped, Regency-cut trouser suit for £7. The black crêpe dress wasn't a very typical Biba dress, except in its shortness (and I may well have taken it up a bit myself). Biba clothes were usually coloured, patterned even, though only in sludgy tones, plums, earthy browns, dusty blues, never anything bright. I found this utterly black dress hanging on one of the coatstands, grabbed the size eight (I'm not sure Biba made anything above a size ten – I couldn't then imagine anyone being above a size ten), and as I stepped into it and watched, as one of my fellow shoppers zipped up the back for me in the multi-mirrored communal dressing room, the floor of which was ankle-deep with discarded items, I saw the image of my marvellous skating girl appear in the icy glass.

~

Growing up is partly about trying on superficial looks to match how you want people to see you, and how you want to see yourself. Controlling how people literally view you is a way of learning to construct a sense of self, until you become confident enough to proceed the other way around. Everyone does it, from the moment they look into a mirror and realise that they can see themselves and therefore other people can see them, and that they have a body which, with a bit of effort, can be brought under the mind's control. It is in the nature of youth to play with style in an effort to come to terms with substance. Easy enough, too, to get stuck there. Narcissism meets the mirror stage and neither condition actually stops in infancy, especially when the times collude. Though there has probably never been a period when young men and women did not look sideways at themselves to catch a glimpse of how they looked to others, the Sixties catered for the concern with the self and how it was to be seen better than most eras, because they coincided with the post-war, post-austerity Western world: a rare island of perceived well-being and a belief in the future as progress, after a long, dark hiatus when no one could be quite sure that the future would not be unimaginably bleak. A time, then, to indulge the children – for a while. A time also for peacetime capitalism to consolidate.

The personal is the political, people began to say, although not until quite a long way into that period designated as the Sixties. But from the start to their end and well beyond, it is truer to say that more than anything for the post-war bulge generation *the personal was the personal*. If the body was to become increasingly regarded as merely the superficial layer outside an infinitely questing mind and spreading social conscience, it was nonetheless, throughout the Sixties, wrapped and tied with the utmost care and attention to detail.

After the war and the austerity years, the means to control how you were seen were newly available to the young. And so was the ability to distinguish yourself visually from your parents. From the Teddy Boys in the Fifties to the Mods and Rockers who took over, and on to the mini-skirted dollybirds of the mid-Sixties and the diaphanous hippies of the later Sixties, many more young people than ever before had, for various reasons, enough money to pay for dramatic self-definition. If they left school at fifteen without qualifications, they found jobs, lost them, found them again, easily earning money while often still living at home. At any rate, there was enough surplus after paying the parents for your keep to buy a long, velvet-collared jacket and drainpipes, a sharp Italian-styled suit, a tiny scrap of a frock from Biba, Bus Stop or even, if you saved up, Bazaar, though only the genuinely well-off could afford any of the painted silks and velvets from Granny Takes A Trip. Those who stayed on at school and went to university were rewarded with enough pocket money or a decent local authority student grant that was designed to be lived on. Even being broke, unemployed and living in a damp bedsitter didn't present an impossible bar to style. The easy availability of social security and the dole are a forgotten but vital factor during the whole of the Sixties, and well into the Seventies. Unconsciously, as it might have been, the welfare system that the newly elected government brought in after the war in order to ensure a fair and just society was also the way in which the older generation were to indulge their post-war children. The Forties turned to the Fifties, the Fifties became the Sixties, and the Sixties seemed to go on for ever, but even then, as the old ones gnashed their teeth and tore out their hair at the goings-on of their wild, rebellious young, they continued to pay them a state stipend, unemployment benefit or a generous student grant, underwriting, as it were, their worst fears. There was always a way to get something you really wanted. Or so it seemed. One trick (with clothes then and relationships later) was to jettison the notion our parents had of the well-made, the built-to-last, the long-term, the good investment. Clothes that were made badly and cheaply didn't last, sometimes not more than a few weeks without coming apart at the seams, but if they had style and wit, it was of no consequence; it was a new way to have what you wanted when you wanted it, and then to have the repeated satisfaction of finding the next new thing. Older people of all classes were horrified at the waste and lack of quality, but that was part of the pleasure for us: to see the shock and disapproval and bafflement in the eyes of the generation who had scraped by and lost all kinds of treasures during the war, and discovered when it was over that they still had to make do and mend: a generation who genuinely valued the patina of age.

If in fact we really only began to develop new kinds of uniform, they were at least dictated by our own generation. The static fashion of our elders was dreary and camouflaging. When we put on the clothes they approved of we automatically looked middle-aged. We rejected the neat pleats and the matching suits, battled against twinsets and pearls, refused in various ways to look respectable – and thereby developed the freedom to look like everyone else under twenty-five. You really couldn't be seen wearing a skirt that was a couple of inches too long. It made you feel wretched. On a camping holiday in Assisi I was persuaded to be sensible and to lower my hem two inches, still short enough for me to be refused entry to the Basilica of St Francis, and felt for the entire two weeks like an old woman shuffling about in widow's weeds. As far as I was concerned, only a properly minuscule skirt could distinguish me from the nuns queuing up to see the Grotto.

I knew well enough my extraordinary good fortune in having a Biba size eight body* and that life was miserable for those who didn't. I knew this because of my hair. After the backcombed beehives of the Fifties and very early Sixties had deflated, only Vidal Sassoon's new geometrically precise version of the 1920s bob – dead straight hair

---

* Though Barbara Hulanicki herself, the actual Biba, imagined that 'everyone' was as thin as a stick because of being the generation born into post-war food shortages. It doesn't seem to have occurred to her that fat girls wouldn't have wanted to suffer the humiliation of not finding anything to fit, or the shame of the communal dressing rooms.

that fell to a knife edge at the jawline – would do. My hair was thick and curly: I ironed it straight, I spent hours rolling it, pulling it painfully as it dried to achieve only a half-hearted version of the desired look that immediately sprang back to catastrophe at the first sign of rain. I was well aware of the dismalness of the never-quite-right. Finally, I gave up and dragged it tightly back so that it was at least sort of invisible and made me look severe enough to seem not to care. My hair caused me misery and shame. Self-presentation didn't diminish as we turned down the legacy of our parents' wardrobes. Very little mattered more than how you looked. Social approval was quite as powerful as it ever had been and has remained. We simply readjusted the idea of whose approval we were after.

And if that was, in retrospect, no different from any other youth cohort, neither was the means by which our style became available to us. All those ground-breaking, cheap and cheerful garments were made in order to fulfil and incite demand, by the same old system that has since the end of feudalism specialised in generating and then granting the wishes of human beings and thereby ruling the world. The clothes were designed and initially made by the young, but they were sold in shops – renamed boutiques: tiny spaces, sometimes, with a handful of dresses or trousers – whose rents had to be paid, where turnover was required, and profits were taken or the shops closed. A new market in boutiques, opening and closing within weeks sometimes, played out a speeded-up capitalism,

which proceeded as it had always done. Youthful entrepreneurs, their vision in sync with their generation,
their ambition the same as generations before them,
offered their contemporaries clothes, music, information and other things to want at the price they could
afford. Richard Branson with the sexily named Virgin
record shops, Felix Dennis at the radical *Oz* magazine
and Tony Elliott's cool listings magazine *Time Out* sold
the young packages that looked like amateurish rejec-
tions of the old way, and seeded their later conventional
media empires. John Stephen opened a little shop called
His Clothes, selling Mod suits in an alley behind Regent
Street in the late Fifties, and to this day tourists wander
down Carnaby Street, soaking up the 'atmosphere'. The
tiny boutique Biba, in Abingdon Road, thrived in 1964
and moved to a much more visible and larger site in Kensington Church Street, then, bigger still, to Kensington
High Street, until it finally over-reached itself (with City
funding), in a veritable parody of capitalism, by taking
over the huge department store Derry & Tom's, selling
bedsheets, paint, kitchenware and cocktails as well as
frocks and maternity dresses, and went bust within two
years.

The economy was booming, finally, and in the first
half of the 1960s, at least, there was no dissent from the
young about the conventionally capitalist manner in
which their desired goods were made available to them.
Nothing much radical was going on here apart from
cheapness and short-termism – hardly anathema to

capitalism. The revolution was a long way off. We were the first generation who could shop till we dropped without anxiety or much regard for the size of our income, and, just like now, our desire for style was catered for by designers, manufacturers, retail outlets, advertisers, public relations companies, photographers, celebrities, models, fashion magazines and financial backers. The taxman was paid, so the state received some of the money. The same old system was operating in the same old manner, doing what it does best: taking advantage of whatever circumstances exist. It is the way of the market. At that early stage we weren't, for the most part, after a different way, just different things. But because we were young, and being catered for so attentively, it felt brand new; and because we were young and are now no longer, we are inclined to remember it as quite different from anything that has happened since.

The art world (no shortage of art schools and grants to attend them for young people who didn't fancy university) joined in the fun and called itself Pop. The word 'popular' in relation to the arts might conceivably have a twang of the radical about it; a bold rejection of the traditionalist understanding of it as meaning a loss of quality. But the diminutive 'pop' merely suggested 'new' and 'fun'. And 'throwaway'. It wasn't confronting, only absorbing, and consuming. If occasionally some works commented on or liberated themselves from this apparent fact of life (Lichtenstein, Warhol, Hockney), they were soon enough reincorporated into commerce.

Warhol's Campbell's Soup tins returned to advertising as advertising itself became the sexiest industry and took all the new talent it could find – photographers, designers, writers, artists, film-makers – to its bosom. Pop Art belonged to the same world as pop music in the early Sixties (the corporate-managed and decidedly unradical Sandie Shaw, Billy J. Kramer, Cilla Black and Dave Clark Five were topping the charts); it was as much about the market as clothes were, and as such became an essential part of our everyday life. Clothes were overprinted with motifs from pictures hanging in galleries, pictures and sculpture reflected passing style (advertising, comics, pornography) and the cheap, throwaway attitudes of fashion that felt so much like fresh air. Record covers became art, art became tea towels. Things got mixed up in a way that was original and amusing to us. Our parents kept things separate and appropriate: art in galleries, certain clothes for particular occasions, work marked off from play, private walled away from public, formal dissociated from casual. Their mores derived from the old rules, the strictures of Leviticus: *Ye shall keep my statutes. Thou shalt not let thy cattle gender with a diverse kind: thou shalt not sow thy field with mingled seed: neither shall a garment mingled of linen and woollen come upon thee.*[2] That ancient terror of mixing things up, of losing the order of things. One thing must be one thing, never another too. Pop Art, in its very shallowness, rejected the old way. Separated, actually, the young from their elders. The freedom to try new things, to play, to incorporate, extended to the arts and bounced back again to daily existence in a quite novel, non-Judaeo-Christian way.

~

Was it *all* only about style and its marketing? Was nothing to be taken seriously in those days up to the mid-Sixties, when London was deemed by *Time* magazine in 1966 to have started 'swinging'? Between the ages of fifteen and eighteen I may have spent an inordinate amount of energy worrying about my hair and shortening my skirts (though not much has changed there, apart from the length of the skirts), but between visits to the mirror other things were impinging on my life. Most of it wasn't quite so brand new, however, as the asymmetric Sassoon cut or a pair of Courrèges boots. Those more cerebral, less sartorial matters that gained my attention during this time were almost entirely developments or continuations of what had been happening in the 1950s and before. The recent war, immediately prior to my birth, I paid almost no attention to, since, being the most vivid years of my parents' life, it was more archaic to me than the English Civil War. But I was powerfully aware of having missed out on the doings of the youthful generation just before mine. While I was still pushing a toy Coronation coach and horses across the living room floor, some very interesting things had been going on in the world outside the four enclosing walls of our small flat in Tottenham Court Road. There weren't just the Teddy

Boys ripping up cinema seats with their flick knives, and people sipping Brown Windsor soup in dismal English dining rooms, there were also the Beats, a Cold War in full frost, and a collapsing British Empire hanging on to its genteel skirts, the results of all of which were beginning to make the rest of the world, no longer merely to be dismissed as 'abroad', look very interesting.

I became aware of the Beats, jazz, poetry, cool, and muddled them properly with the existentialism of Sartre and Camus' fiction while I was at boarding school, mixing with the wrong crowd from the local town who had designated a corporation bench near a roundabout just outside the centre the 'Beat Seat'. There we sat while they, older than me – in their late teens while I was thirteen and fourteen – told me to read the books any self-respecting wannabe Beat had to know. *Jude the Obscure*, *Ulysses*, *Crime and Punishment*. Not bad reading recommendations as bad-friends go. I found *Lolita* for myself, listened to *Red Bird*, poetry and modern jazz from Christopher Logue via Pablo Neruda, and discovered that in America some, like Allen Ginsberg, were already howling most ungenteelly about the state of the world. If it was a little downbeat, that was fine by me. I was already angry and sullen – a gift from my dysfunctional family, as well as, doubtless, a dash of biochemistry – and ready to argue with any form of authority that came my way. Just before I was fifteen, I was expelled from the co-educational, progressive boarding school the local council had paid for me to attend in order to improve my character and absent me from my mother – not for reading those books, but for sniffing ether, and getting caught after attending an all-night party. In various ways, I was the Sixties waiting to happen.

After the Beat Seat and expulsion, my Sixties continued in a psychiatric hospital near Brighton, but in 1963 I went back to live in London, invited by the mother of a former fellow-pupil, who, the following year, sent me to another school, where the plan was to do my O and A levels and become, in spite of the educational blip, one of those of my generation who went to university. It seemed, after a somewhat turbulent childhood, fairly straightforward. But I took the book-and-poetry reading and the anger along with me to London. There was still an awful lot of reading to catch up on, some terrible poetry to write, and I also discovered, in the culturally rich atmosphere of the house I had fetched up in, a world of film. Not that films were new to me. My childhood block of flats was attached to a cinema. Movies were at my back door. I went to everything I could get into, as well as finding cunning, illegal routes into those I was forbidden by law to see. They were westerns, soupy romances, Fifties comedies and British B movies. Now I filled in the gaps of the past at the National Film Theatre, going to classic silents and Hollywood marvels of the Thirties and Forties. In addition, there was an entirely new cinema to me, from Europe and beyond, to discover. Godard, Fellini, Antonioni, Bergman, Kurosawa, Ozu, Ray, Truffaut, Malle, Pasolini, Polanski, Jiri Menzel.

They mattered enough for me to take illicit afternoons off school in order to get to the first matinée showing of *8½* or *The Silence* at the crucial Academy Cinema in Oxford Street, where I'd sit in the smoky auditorium with fifteen or so other film fanatics, and one or two flashers, overwhelmed by the potent sexual narratives and social critiques, Marxist, psychoanalytic, libertarian or simply different and, to me, astonishing. I absorbed the complexities of relationship, and spiritual or cultural emptiness, played out in tones of grey, with echoes of poets, writers and philosophers. Godard's intensely charming, hopeless and crazy about love film, *Pierrot Le Fou*, had me returning eight times during its run. I couldn't take my eyes off a single frame, or miss one step of Monica Vitti's slow, despairing walks through the blighted urban wasteland in Antonioni's *Red Desert*. I wept sometimes with exaltation, sometimes rage, at the visions coming at me from the Academy screen. And, let me say, all this lived quite easily with my despair at my unsatisfactory hair and concern for the precise shortness of my skirt.

There was music, too. Older friends introduced me to Mozart and Beethoven string quartets, opera, Brecht and Weill. I discovered Ives and Copland. And, of course, all the while listened to pirate radio, Caroline and London, and watched *Ready Steady Go* and *Top of the Pops* religiously. Buddy Holly, Roy Orbison, the Everly Brothers, the Beach Boys, the Four Tops, Pete Seeger, Joan Baez, Bob Dylan, John Coltrane, Miles Davis, Thelonius Monk, Charlie Mingus, the Beatles (though I was disdainful until *Rubber Soul* came along), the Stones, the Animals, the Kinks, all either accompanied me from the beginning of the decade or had emerged by the middle of it and were essential: the rhythm inside my head, the beat of my heart, the tuning of my sentiments.

~

The Fifties are often characterised by a lack of colour. Like most of the movies, they were, everyone agrees, in black and white. In memory, the streets, the clothes, the prospects of the Fifties were in shades of grey. The arrival of colour was no more than implied in the early Sixties. The boldness, at first, was all about the insistent use of monochrome. Black and white was style, art and commentary. Aubrey Beardsley reproductions decorated walls and Bridget Riley paintings shimmered into fabric, Richard Avedon took pictures documenting the civil rights movement and mental hospital patients, David Bailey portrayed the rich and the influential. All of it in a kind of mockery of the 1950s lack of colour. Each of them using the dramatic contrast of black and white, or the grey tones between as a bridge from where we had been to where we were going. White lips, black eyes; implacable black dress, white Courrèges cut-out boots. Bergman, Antonioni, Pasolini. All of this spoke of the colour that wasn't there, of an absence that until then we hadn't really noticed. All that insistent black and white screamed the lack of colour that we had put up with and worked its way into forms of art and expression. Colour was possible before the Sixties, but it took time before the world needed to be represented by the full spectrum. Did colour explode into being with the increasing use of drugs? Or did the stark simplicity of black and white finally pall? The middle Sixties was that moment when Dorothy stepped through her front door, out of Kansas, on to the undreamed-of yellowness of the brick road on the way to the Emerald City, and the heart burst with pleasure at the sudden busting out of a full-blown Technicolor world.

Pop and culture came together for people of my age who had encouragement and the opportunity to explore. It was always the case that middle-class young people were able to discover the arts if they were so inclined, but now the stuff that was coming at all young people from youth-oriented popular media pointed to other things and mixed it all up so much more than had happened before.

The Campaign for Nuclear Disarmament and the more militant Committee of 100 were political organisations devoted to unilateral nuclear disarmament. But the Aldermaston March and the sit-down demonstrations organised by the Committee of 100 became culturally and socially desirable for the young who wanted not only to create a sense of peace and security for the world but also to meet each other and rebel against the elders. Our parents, and the papers they read, hated the marchers with their long hair, jeans, resistance songs and clashes with the police. What more could an angry fifteen-year-old want? I had waited, along with the rest of the world, to be blown to pieces on 11–12 October 1962. While I sat on the snowy pebble beach watching the grim-grey sea in Brighton, America and Russia played chicken in what became known as the Cuban Missile Crisis. It wasn't history happening at the time – it was perfectly clear to me, and to others, that my world was very likely to end within forty-eight hours. There seemed every reason, once I got to London and my liberal new household, to join in the marches and sit down in the street. There was also the promise of tens of thousands of people of my age and older, like-minded, looking scruffy and cool, having, as the *Daily Mail* and the *People* promised, sex like rabbits, and really annoying, actually scaring, vast numbers of the majority we were so intent on being different from. I had ached to go when I was under my parents' control and couldn't. When I finally set off on my first Aldermaston in 1963, it was my version of the debutantes' coming-out ball.

Along with anger and style, mockery was another way to identify who we were and who we were not. Satire revived, and even those who considered themselves the majority sat down every Saturday night to watch *That Was the Week That Was*, either to huff and puff about the loss of respect or to cheer on the biting opposition to the abominable, reactionary Tory Home Secretary, Henry Brooke, the Cold War and the new Labour government's collusion in the American war in Vietnam. Astonishing things had happened in the US. Over there, people of our age had grown up with nuclear drill, learning how to crouch under their desks in case of a nuclear attack. America became a synonym for violence and structural racism. Kennedy was killed, then Martin Luther King, another Kennedy and Malcolm X as the struggle for civil rights began to gather momentum, and radical student movements of the Left both in America and in Europe started to make themselves known. The Vietnam war drafted people of our age into a monstrous and unjust battle. Less violently but just as angrily, Bob Dylan went electric in 1965, and the early skirmishes commenced between the pure and the down and dirty of popular music. America was the beginning of all things new and forthcoming to parochial Britain, swinging as it might have been, and it seemed, looking across the Atlantic, as if the world was wobbling on its axis. It was dangerous, but it was exciting. It felt as if it was not just our time, my time as a young person, but that it was like no time ever before. A snowball had started its progress and had rolled hugely towards the generation born after the Second World War. Us, me. It was full of promise, and we developed an increasing sense of responsibility to use our time of being young – to indulge ourselves, golden generation that we were, but also to give warning that when our lot grew to be old enough to take charge, things were going to be radically, *radically* different.

2

ALTERING REALITIES

And the ones that mother gives you
Don't do anything at all…
                    Jefferson Airplane, 'White Rabbit'

Drugs: my mother in the 1950s standing at the window of our fifth-floor flat clutching a huge white cardboard box of soluble codeine and aspirin tablets. She got them from the doctor on prescription, 100 at a time. Headaches. Later, early in 1962, when I was fifteen, I ran away from my father to her bedsitting room in Hove, where she had a much smaller box containing Nembutal on the chest of drawers. Insomnia. There were eight left in it when I swallowed them a couple of days later, certain that we couldn't survive each other in the tiny room, and that there was and never would be anywhere else to go. Not enough to kill me, but sufficient, it turned out, to get me out of the room, into the care of a hospital and away from both parents for good.

Before that I had been in Banbury with my father, working in a series of shops on the high street, not allowed to go back to school as punishment for my expulsion. At first I'd stolen the ether from the school chemistry lab, then bought it in bottles from local chemists, telling them it was for killing butterflies. I can't remember how I knew about sniffing ether – the only prohibited drug used at the school in those days was tobacco – but when I tried it I was entranced – precisely – by the immensity of the time I seemed to have been unconscious in a fathomless and dreameasy world. I liked the aeons away from *real* it gave me, though in reality it was only minutes. But it wasn't very long before the endless nether etherworld became inhabited by monsters. An eternity of bad dreams was not what I was after at all.

Five years later, and in another hospital, not the one in Hove they sent me to after the Nembutal overdose, I discovered methylamphetamine – Methedrine. I was nineteen or twenty and a fellow patient shared a glass ampoule of it with me and showed me how to use a syringe to skin-pop into a muscle. Time stretched out again, marvellously, though now without a loss of consciousness. Thoughts paraded in front of me like actors taking their bows on stage, stopping for a time to be considered and then passing on. I watched them while I sat back, my favourite way of being in the world, as audience to my own but autonomous mind. A time-traveller's way of inhabiting my own interior. I liked that very much. A lot better than the coal gas we bubbled through milk in the patients' kitchen to get a cheap and available high.

A year later, in a third psychiatric hospital, the Maudsley, I was admitted by the dour Dr Krapl Taylor, who told me that I was a typical addictive personality, and (in a strange non-sequitur) that he would treat my depressed, disordered personality with – I couldn't believe my luck – Methedrine therapy. Twice a week I saw his crew-cut houseman, who injected Methedrine directly into my vein and then set about trying to get me to 'abreact'. The idea was to make me distressed enough to have a crisis, which, magically, like a fever breaking, was supposed to relieve me of my depression. 'You're worthless,' he would tell me. 'I know,' I'd say. 'Can I have some more Methedrine, please?'

Eventually, I left the Maudsley in a rage (abreacting, you might say) and found my way to the much-talked-of Arts Lab in Drury Lane. Upstairs in the café, above the exhibition space (Yoko Ono, I think, a little-known avant-garde artist), I turned around in my chair and said to the man who happened to be behind me, 'Do you know where I can get some Methedrine?' He did. I had found one of the speed kings of central London, it turned out, and for a while (until the Methedrine high got very much worse than the ether horrors) I mainlined the stuff. I moved into a flat in Long Acre in Covent Garden in which friends of my dealer lived and found myself my first home, at home as I had never experienced it before. Even as a small child with my parents, I had felt like I was in the wrong place with the wrong people. Now, I sat cross-legged on the floor with my back to the wall and watched the thoughts dancing across my brain, in a smoky room of stoned strangers or friends I'd known for only weeks, and in a way that was completely new to me, I was at last where I really belonged.

Of course, I smoked dope, too. I always had a joint ready-rolled by the bed for first thing in the morning, and couldn't imagine a time – when I tried to picture a future – when I would not smoke cannabis. It seemed ridiculous to choose not to be stoned. I also dropped acid, though with much more trepidation than any of the other drugs I used. I was sure, the first time I sucked on an LSD-soaked sugar cube, that it would be the end of me. I knew my depressive tendencies. I had had bad trips even on cannabis. The ether and the Methedrine had turned nasty. I was certain that my chances of becoming irredeemably psychotic on acid were very high. I said a serious goodbye to myself as I put the sugar cube on my tongue.

Nonetheless, I took it. Was it because taking a risk was worth the marvellous insights I believed I would get if the trip happened to go the other way? Or, more likely, because risk was by definition good, or at any rate necessary? There was no choice but to take whatever risk was on offer. Or perhaps it was because I really didn't care whether I was mad or sane, or more accurately, alive or dead? It's hard to say, but during that time I was also taking Seconal capsules (a barbiturate, like Nembutal) all day and night, a high dose, prescribed, every four hours. I had discovered another way with Seconal, and sometimes injected myself with it in solution, the effect of which was instant and vacant unconsciousness. There was no other pleasure to be had out of shooting it, except the rush of blankness that filled me up the instant the Seconal hit my brain. I was after exactly that blankness, and also as importantly that millisecond of knowledge that I was becoming unconscious. It certainly wasn't the permanent madness that a bad trip threatened. But apparently even the risk of madness was preferable to being on nothing at all.

~

No one thought of the drug-taking as ' recreational'. That was a later concept. Even if my particular bent for self-negation was untypical, the drug-taking young of the Sixties I lived with and met also took their drugs very seriously. Not that we didn't have fun, but having fun wasn't recreational. We didn't do recreation. Well, we didn't do work very much. At our most pompous we told ourselves that we worked at finding out how best or better to be alive. But however we justified it, we really didn't make the distinction between work and recreation that shaped our parents' daily existence. We didn't have to, because, to reiterate, one way or another the State was paying for us to study or take paid work (waitressing in the café in the Arts Lab, dealing hash, bookshop assist-ant, selling the *International Times*) very lightly. There was no need to worry, as our parents did on our behalf, about 'getting on', because we had no plan to live in a world in which getting on was of any importance. If there was a plan at all, it was precisely to prevent such a world from structuring our future. We were brainstorming ways of destructuring everything to suit ourselves. We were almost grown-ups, it was inevitable that the world would become fully ours eventually, and therefore, with ourselves in charge, it would be completely different.

We were certainly not in the majority, not even in our own generation. There were far more 'straight' young people than those of us living self-consciously outside the law, dotted about London as well as most other towns and cities in the country. There were enough of us to produce underground papers to pass the news around, to fill the Roundhouse so that we could celebrate the crowd we made, to keep headshops selling pipes and joint papers, and bookshops like Indica and Compendium, busy if not in profit. But, of course, most people took on the world as it was offered to them. This is always the case. Possibly apart from the generations that came to adulthood around the start of the First and Second World Wars, most people aren't actively engaged in what any given era is later characterised by. Not everyone in France was fomenting revolution in 1789; only a tiny proportion of the new generation were Bright Young Things of the 1920s. What may have been different by 1967 was how easy it was to opt out of the world of adults and yet find ready-made social networks to support our dissent. That the majority chose not to, made them, in our eyes, wilfully blind. The world was in fact going on as it always had, but it seemed to me and the people I knew that it had no idea what it was in for.

The Stones' two-and-a-half-minute sneer, 'Mother's Little Helper', accurately reflected the way in which we turned our backs on the 'straights'. We didn't take drugs to get by, we took drugs to see the world entirely differently. The straight world had our contempt. It wasn't drugs as such that separated us and them. It was the kind of drugs and the reason for taking them. The Valium-popping wives isolated from reality, trying to keep up with phantom materialism in their suburban villas on Acacia Road or any of the other suitably pastorally referenced streets. The differently isolated working-class women who were also being dished out prescription tranquillisers, to help them cope with their children on the twentieth floor of the high-rise council blocks that were springing up everywhere. Those who colluded with stasis brought about their own doom. We were doing something with drugs, they were just surviving the intolerable world that they had either created or acquiesced in.

Our youthful cruelty was boundless. Youth does cruelty quite easily, not having the accretions of time to deal with, but I remember a glaring clarity as I looked at the bourgeois life and its compromises, the working life and its compliance, and what seemed the direct consequences of both, that may have demanded cruelty to reassure ourselves that we could stay clear of it. Some of the generation that had come to their young adulthood in the Fifties had seen it too and hit the road. It's a kind of laser-guided vision, a pure beam of light in a crepuscular landscape, that is available to the young when they look at the world that has been made ready for them, which they are about to step out into. You see it in your children when they get that pitying, disdainful smile on their face and don't bother to argue with you because you can't possibly grasp what they know. Which is, simply, that they are new and you are old, and that what they see is being seen accurately for the first time ever. And they are right. The compromises that adults make cause much of the suffering in the world, or, at best, fail to deal with the suffering. Acceptance of one's lot, maintaining a silence about what can't be said, lowering your expectations for your own life and for others, and understanding that nothing about the way the world works will ever change, is the very marrow of maturity, and no wonder the newly-fledged children look at it with horror and know that it won't happen to them – or turn their backs on it for fear it will. They know it's too late for you to 'get it', so they smile and leave the room, away from your reasoning, well, actually, increasingly shrill voice. It's unnerving – especially if you remember that same smile on your own face when you were young. Not everyone, of course not everyone, but that terrible clarity of vision is available to the young of every generation, and those who look become the trouble-makers, the difficult ones, that the elders complain about eternally.

In the second half of the Sixties, if you were of the party that chose to look, you were either hell-bent on getting out of that world, as I perhaps was, or you were going to re-vision it and live the vision. Drugs were just one means, like a spaceship or a spell, of getting through the fog of what 'they' called reality. A presently available technology for bypassing what they assumed was the ine-luctable way of the world. It seemed pellucidly obvious that it could, with a bit of effort, become our way of our world, of a kind we chose to live the rest of our lives in, not theirs. It was necessary, therefore, like explor-ers through the centuries who mapped routes to new worlds, to make extreme, ill-considered efforts to find it. I say this with a slight smile aged sixty in 2008. There were, in fact, many moments when it felt exactly like that in the flat in Covent Garden in 1968. Smiling gently on your younger self is one way of dealing with the astonish-ing lack of change. Timothy Leary describes the knowl-edge we had that the time had come 'for far-out visions, knowing that America had run out of philosophy, that a new, empirical, tangible metaphysics was desperately needed, knowing in our hearts that the old mechanical myths had died at Hiroshima, that the past was over, that politics could not fill the spiritual vacuum…Politics, religion, economics, social structure are based on shared states of consciousness. The cause of social conflict is usually neurological. The cure is biochemical.'[3]

It was easy to be seduced away from a politics which had palpably failed – even a just war had failed to provide peace, and those who had saved the world from Hitler had not prevented the next horror signalled by the nuclear bombs dropped on Japan. In 1967, if you looked around, you saw the continuing confrontation of East and West, the Berlin Wall still standing, mass starvation in Biafra, race riots in the States, the war in Vietnam.

Fear, hunger, deprivation, the oppression by the strong of the weak. Nothing had changed, for all that we were told how a generation had sacrificed its youth in order to make a decent world for us. And even if that were true, how could that generation sit back with a sense of a job well done when terrible things were happening to people all over the planet? In any case, it is not the job of the young to be grateful, it is their job to tear up the world and start again.

What happened when you smoked a joint and to a far greater extent when you dropped acid was that the world outside your head was utterly changed. It looked, I and others would say over and over again as we tripped, so *real*. By which, I suppose, we must have meant *unreal*, except that is not how it seemed. We watched reality become a conundrum as the chemicals we ingested altered the chemicals in our brains. Change and reality were as easy to make and unmake as swallowing a pill or drawing smoke into our lungs. The 'one pill makes you larger, one pill makes you small' of Jefferson Airplane's 'White Rabbit' was a perfect description of the astonishment at the changes we made happen inside our own heads. We had a childlike wonder that we could produce such weirdness from ourselves – that our own familiar minds had the latent capacity to see the world entirely anew. Drugs were also an unfathomable, fascinating, magical toy – it wasn't coincidental that we took to blowing bubbles though plastic hoops and making morphing patterns in bright colours with oil and heat.

And notice how taking acid dripped on to sugar cubes or blotting paper combined the magical contraption with the favoured, forbidden foodstuffs of our childhoods.

There were still books to read, but now they were the *Vedas, Gita, The Tibetan Book of the Dead*, the *I Ching*, books on Buddhism by Alan Watts and D. T. Suzuki, novels and essays informed by Eastern philosophy or drug use by Herman Hesse, Aldous Huxley, Carlos Castaneda, Jack Kerouac and Allen Ginsberg, as well as John Lilly, writing from his sensory deprivation tanks, and Dr Leary, the professor of psychedelia. This reality game, we discovered, had been played for millennia by other cultures with and without the use of drugs. We read up on oriental religions and philosophies and discovered how the West had got it so wrong, and that 'Oh, wow, it's so *real*' was not a brand new vision brought about by brand new chemicals at all. All along Buddhism had been saying that reality was not what it seemed, and the tribal societies had chewed and smoked natural substances that took them into the dream country and gave them stories and visions with which to blur the edges of reality and shift gear out of the mundane. It turned out we hadn't discovered the fast route to re-visioning the world, but we freely partook of its current availability. We had rediscovered it for ourselves, reinvented the point of the prayer wheel and the joint, and were bringing it home. We were investigating and disturbing the self in order to dismiss self. Transformation was our task, change outside from alteration inside. We did it from books: *Teach Yourself*

Altered Consciousness was our generation's virtual addition to that series of practical self-education books we'd grown up with. We knew the worth of self-education. To start with we eschewed the shaman, the guide, the guru – though soon there would be a great flocking to the East in search of teachers and a stream of teachers heading in the other direction towards these willing students. We just took the drugs and read books. There was a feeling that we could, that we had to do it ourselves. Gurus and guides were just another form of parent. We could take the ancient wisdom in its raw form, mix it with lysergic acid diethylamide, and make it work for ourselves. Like those Victorian, Edwardian and post-war children our parents had thought quaint and safe for bedtime reading, we took ourselves off, made our own way, like Alice, Dorothy, the Pevensies and Peter Pan, to different realities, and assumed with the bravado of youth that we'd make it back to Kansas to tell of what we saw and be able to implement the, by definition valuable, new connections and disconnections our changed minds had made.

It's very hard to look at the drug culture here and in the States today from the point of view of those who lived through the Sixties, and understand it as anything other than negative and destructive. The supply and demand has become a template for capitalism. It was always the case that drugs were brought in from somewhere else by entrepreneurs and were divided up to be sold by individuals, and some of those individuals were certainly businessmen. But the grimness and the profiteering have become universal. Watch *The Wire* and you are confronted by the parodic vision of capitalism working perfectly in the projects and high rises. We bequeathed heroin and cocaine to the miserable masses, not any kind of psychedelic solution to poverty and injustice. Luckier kids take Es and party, dance in a trance, and it must be fun – they even call it being 'loved up', but it doesn't seem to have any other cultural aspect attached to it. No books or art, and the music is too mechanical for the likes of my generation to get. The punks were the last comprehensible youth movement, and were a genuine phenomenon for only a flash. And of course, the Sixties drug generation had to watch Thatcher's babies, the thirty-somethings who dealt in fantasy money, hoovering up cocaine just to keep them on a money-making high. It feels to me, although I know that plenty of people were fucked up by drugs back then, that the party has turned spectacularly nasty and pointless.

~

We were also a bunch of dissolute, hedonistic druggies. We lay around and got stoned, had sex, listened to music that exalted lying around, getting stoned, having sex, and hymned our good times. Jefferson Airplane, the Doors, Captain Beefheart, the Grateful Dead, Love, Hendrix, Country Joe and the Fish, Frank Zappa all played our tune from far away on the West Coast of the United States. Their albums arrived in British shops, we bought them, put the records on our turntables, rolled our joints on the covers. We even had some of our own, though it was a little softer, lacking the desperate edge of the Americans. Pink Floyd, the Who, the Stones, the Beatles, the Incredible String Band, the Small Faces, the Animals. The music knew where we were going in our heads and wrote the score. We partied. Perhaps the music was too good, enabling us to stay indoors and just watch and listen. We altered the world hardly at all because, whatever we told each other, and however connected we might have felt sitting in the same room, the search we were on was for the singular, individual experience. To be sure, it was of the interior kind, the kind you can keep still and have, rather than the current much-desired extreme sports, falling-fast-out-of-the-sky sort. But we had about as much effect on the world as someone jumping from a plane does. The straight world wondered what we were up to. They disapproved, they feared, they sent the cops round, and that was all grist to our other sense that we were doing something. But our interior-ity, our single focus on our inner selves did not achieve anything very much. No new ideas, no great books or paintings or poetry come to mind from those late Sixties days – just an album cover or two. And though the music was remarkable, and much of it was recorded in a haze of cannabis smoke, it was usually mixed by sober techni-cians and distributed by multinational companies.

'That's your problem, man...' This telling phrase was used to resolve disputes that arose when love and harmony and the new reality failed to get the washing-up done, or the bath cleaned. It was spoken in a tone of voice that meant something like: each of us has to take responsibility for our own soul's contentment and not impose our constraints on others – man. In the quotidian event it meant that those who wanted a bit of order in the kitchen had to do the washing-up for those who left their dirty plates in the sink. The day-to-day-ness never once looked like another way of being, except, of course, that we didn't go regularly to work or to war. In America at this time, matters were more serious. The music and the drugs were made for and taken into the war zone in order to make the insufferable tolerable, or to remind combatants that their intolerable existence was someone else's fault. In the United Kingdom, however much we tried to empathise, and this is the vital difference between our experience and theirs, our memories of that time and theirs, we had only a generational war to fight.

~

Like children we played cops and robbers and cowboys and Indians in Covent Garden. It involved a lot of cleaning. It may have been my most domesticated period. Whenever there was a rumour of a drugs bust – which was several times a week – floors had to be hurriedly but very thoroughly vacuumed, and surfaces wiped down to catch the bits of hash and grass that had dropped while we made the joints or our friendly dealer cut an ounce from his block. I knew people who had been busted for a speck of hash that the vacuum cleaner had missed. For those who actually went to prison – one twenty-five-year-old I knew for two years for having a couple of grams – playtime stopped. But for most of us, we acted out our underground lives, developed paranoia and outlaw slang with all the solemn delight of Peter Pan's lost boys. It was a dangerous game. There were people who didn't stop injecting Methedrine when it started to go bad. Drug doctors did the rounds of certain flats and wrote out private prescriptions for whole cartons of Burroughs Wellcome's blue and white 12-ampoule boxes. People went crazy, got very ill. There is no describing the come-down from a long weekend on Methedrine. I stopped it when I started to see bugs crawling about all over me and couldn't catch them. But for a few weeks I lived with a much healthier, more disciplined heroin addict. We shared the kitchen of the flat in Covent Garden. A mattress on the floor, covered with a gold candlewick bedspread to make it more homely. In that period addicts were registered with a licensed general practitioner or clinic, and received from them controlled amounts of heroin. It meant that they could be physically and mentally monitored and, although there was some over-prescription, there wasn't a great surplus of heroin on the market. This policy was stopped in 1975. In 1971 there were between 6,000 and 15,000 drug users; by 2002 the number had risen to between 161,000 and 266,000. In 1968 the great days of the entrepreneurial drug industry were yet to come, and there was also no organised crime involvement; the black market was mostly from over-prescription by doctors. If you needed heroin you got it for nothing. My boyfriend made his daily rounds, visiting the doctor, the chemist, shooting up regularly, and felt vastly superior to us outlaws. He disapproved of doing drugs. He was sick, he told us when we rolled a joint or dropped acid. We were just messing about. He dressed neatly and with care, washed his hair daily, made sure he ate nourishing food regularly, and kept his equipment tidy in a black leather zip-up case which he carried with him everywhere. He went out each morning and did who knew what, wheeling and dealing, bartering and selling things and sometimes part of his prescription, but not breaking into houses or mugging people on the street for a fix.

When he left for the day, I tidied up, returning our private bedroom to the kitchen everyone in the flat used. I made the bed and put away the apple box we had as a bedside table. When he came home, the morning syringe he had left by the bed was clean. I washed out the drops of blood and drug residue every morning at the sink after I'd washed up the teacups, sluiced it thoroughly with boiled water, taking it apart and leaving it on the drainer to dry. It wasn't until some weeks into my daily morning routine that I noticed any similarity between my domestic activities and the suburban pill-popping housewives I was never going to become like. Of course, this was a panto version. We played our serious mind-enhancing

games, and we played pirates, but like children everywhere we also played house.

3

BODY WORK

> We had these appetites that we understood and it was
> wonderful that they were taken care of. It was a moment
> where everybody was giving to the other person what
> they wanted. The women knew that's what the men
> wanted.
>
> Interview with Leonard Cohen
> in the *Globe and Mail*, Weekend Review, Canada, 26 May 2007

> People fucked back then just as much as they do now. We
> just didn't talk about it as much.
>
> Henry Miller in the film *Reds*, 1981

In 1973 I was teaching at a girls' state comprehensive school in Hackney, East London. One day after an English lesson with a class of fourteen-year-olds, a girl stayed behind to speak to me. She looked very awkward, near to tears, surprising because she was an outspoken, knowing young woman.

'What's up?'

It took her a while to explain, or for me to understand exactly what the problem was. She didn't know what to do, she said. What about? Well, she'd put a Tampax in, you know, inside her, when she got her period last week. And? The string, she didn't know how, but the string sort of went up, too. She forgot to pull it out first, she supposed. And? Well, what should she do? About what?

Finally, it dawned on me.

'You mean it's still in there? After a week?'

'Yes, Miss. I don't know what to do. Should I go to the doctor?'

I still hadn't got the problem.

'Just take it out.'

'But I can't. The string's not there.'

'Put your fingers into your vagina and take it out.'

Her face changed from worry to pure disgust.

'What, put my fingers up inside me? I'm not touching myself there. Miss!'

The next day I brought my copy of *Our Bodies, Ourselves* by the Boston Women's Health Collective into school and left it in an unlocked cupboard in my room. It described women's and men's bodies, how they worked, what they did, how they did it, in straightforward language with simple drawings and photographs. The coffee-table-sized paperback, a US import, became so dog-eared and smudged with page-turning and fingermarks I had to replace it every couple of terms with a new copy. I'd arrive in my classroom after break and lunch to see knots of girls already there, crowded round one of the tables and the book open in front of them.

This, as I say, was in 1973. Long after the *Lady Chatterley* ban and the Beatles' first LP. People may well have fucked freely back in the early twentieth century, and even for Philip Larkin sexual intercourse had started ten years previously, as indeed it probably had already for many of the girls poring over the book, but in 1973 in Hoxton, London, a fourteen-year-old young woman who used the word 'fuck' like a comma, told smutty jokes and almost certainly knew what a penis looked and felt like had been walking around with a week-old tampon inside her because it was 'dirty' to put her fingers into her vagina.

~

The year before I had helped to set up a free school for some local hardcore truants, which was eventually funded by Camden Council and sited in one of several sheds in an old soon-to-be-built-on freightliner depot, along with a youth club, an old people's lunch club and a women's centre. After a few weeks, there were complaints from the women's centre that the free school kids were breaking in to their shed at night. Nothing was taken, nothing damaged, apart from the door lock and the light left on all night. We asked the kids about it. Yeah, they said, the boys, anyway. There was this poster stuck on the wall of the women's centre. They'd broken in to look at it. What was it? Shrugs. Y'know. Nope, don't know. What was it? No one would say. We went to look, and saw on the wall, opposite a window, a two foot by two foot colour poster, all pinks, reds and purples, of a vulva, spread wide open, showing the labia and entrance to the vagina. At the time, women's groups were keen on investigating their own bodies. They examined their sexual parts with the aid of speculums, mirrors and their friends, familiarising themselves with what was felt to have been appropriated by men for their own private gaze. The free school boys, children and young adolescents, wanted to see as well.

'What did you do?'

'Looked at it.'

'Is that all?'

'Well, we jerked off. Obviously.'

It did seem obvious, speaking to them. The women were furious. They were being violated, they said. We explained this to the free school kids.

'Well,' one of them said. 'I'd never seen one just there on a wall like that before. What else you supposed to do with it? What do they expect?'

It was an interesting point, and quite a fruitful discussion began about the nature of different points of view of a single subject. The boys went to the woman in charge and apologised for breaking in. They weren't well received. If it happened again, she was going to call the police. The women's centre and the free school kids never did see eye to eye.

~

Taking off our clothes was an important part of the project of undoing the constraints we perceived our elders to have been immobilised by. We stripped conscientiously in front of each other and made nothing of it. Sex was written about and acted out in private and public with enthusiasm in the name of the sexual revolution. The idea was to have fun, because having fun with our bodies was a completely new way of being with our peers. Of course we were young and therefore taking our clothes off was relatively unproblematic, because what we saw was on the whole easy to look at. We scorned covering ourselves up for any other reason than aesthetics – and warmth. Clothes (except the beautiful, floaty, diaphanous kind that invited the slightest zephyr to puff them away) were an obstacle to the freedom of bodies, and also signified the draping of the mind. In 1973 – the early Seventies, a seminal period it seems for discovering that not so much had changed – Erica Jong's heroine Isadora Wing[4] had finally defined what it was the Sixties generation were in search of, and evidently still hadn't found. It was 'the zipless fuck'. It seemed to be several things all at once, not all of them compatible: it was wildly romantic, a teen dream of you didn't quite know what glimpsed frustratingly in vague erotic prose and on movie screens:

> Zipless because when you came together zippers fell away like rose petals, underwear blew off in one breath like dandelion fluff. Tongues intertwined and turned liquid. Your whole soul flowed out through your tongue and into the mouth of your lover.

It was also emotionally utopian. Free from the complexities of possessive responses trained by the rigid, repressive social apparatus that caused the Fifties generation to moulder, as we saw it, in sexual frustration. All done up in tight-waisted, hobble-skirted, corseted clothing and manners.

> The zipless fuck is absolutely pure. It is free of ulterior motives. There is no power game . The man is not 'taking' and the woman is not 'giving.' No one is attempting to cuckold a husband or humiliate a wife. No one is trying to prove anything or get anything out of anyone. The zipless fuck is the purest thing there is. And it is rarer than the unicorn. And I have never had one.

The reality of the zipless fuck was as far removed from romance as it was possible to get. That was the point:

> For the true, ultimate zipless A-1 fuck, it was necessary that you never get to know the man very well…. So another condition for the zipless fuck was brevity. And anonymity made it even better.

Of course, the zipless fuck absolutely required the pill, without which fumbling and anxiety, no matter how advanced the mind might be, was unavoidable. It was invented in 1961, but was available only to married women or those brave enough to get a cheap ring from Woolworths and brazen it out in grim family planning clinics. Between 1962 and 1969, the number of users in the UK rose from approximately 50,000 to one million. It helped not to have to rely on men to use condoms properly or withdraw at the right moment, or have to remember to put in the diaphragm before, but not too long before, it was likely you were going to have sex. It was a great advance for women in general, worldwide, even for the cause of sexual liberation. But the fact that Isadora was still looking for this unencumbered encounter in 1973, and that women found *Fear of Flying* a compelling read, tells us a lot about the difficulty of achieving the sexual revolution we had been trying so hard for. The post-war generation was brought up by parents who aimed for respectability, and to conceal any suggestion that the body was not under the strict control of the civilised mind. The great weapons were shame and embarrassment. It was not only difficult to find yourself unmarried and pregnant (bringing up children is at any period a very tough one-person activity), it was a disgrace. Hiding the fact was far more important than dealing with it. Our parents, a generation that had responded to the uncertainty of war with a good deal of sexual licence (the writer John Mortimer remembered VE Day, when the grassy expanses of Hyde Park heaved with copulating couples), and during the bombings and enforced separations snatched physical pleasure in the face of absence and death, now scurried back to the social straight and narrow and impressed on its children the need to conform. Working-class or middle-class, respectability, in the sense of not doing anything the neighbours didn't want you to think they did, was a very high priority.

The sexual revolution is certainly an idea people have about the Sixties. It was also an idea that the Sixties had about itself even though there was, as Henry Miller said, nothing new about small groups of usually affluent or arty people having complicated, delightful and miserable sex with each other. Screwing, joyfully or grimly or even obediently, like rabbits, as if there were no tomorrow. Sex is presumably always a brand new discovery to every generation. A secret they had better not tell their parents about, in case, God forbid, they take it up. In some periods this has happened in spite of the parents doing their damnedest to keep it a secret not just from their children but also from themselves. The Fifties was not an optimum time for sexual openness. Books that had any bearing on the subject were banned or not published without much challenge. It was very hard to get any information about the body. Ignorance and received morality were believed to stroll hand in hand, just like back before we were cast out of the garden. This time it was back gardens and yards with fences just the right height to gossip over. In any case, in the Fifties, England was not conducive in a practical way to bodily delight. Houses were cold and damp, with no central heating. Bathrooms were grim, icy affairs of chilled, cracking lino and uncertain waterheaters that gave up their hot water, after a good deal of clanking and groaning, in a thin stream that was inclined to run cold when the money in the gas meter ran out long before the bath was more than a puddle. The spa experience was a long way off. The sensual pleasures of steaming scented wet-rooms where bodies were (worth it, worth it) deservedly pampered, muscles relaxed, skin moisturised in preparation for a night of love of self or other, alone or in company, was too remotely in the future even to daydream about in the draughty washrooms of 1957. When you'd brushed your teeth and washed your face, you stripped off your clothes and pulled on your nightdress or pyjamas and dived into bed as quickly as you possibly could. Hot water bottle. Eiderdown. Being naked just meant being cold well into the mid-Sixties. Hard to tell if people made love under the covers out of primness or protection against the frost.

Language was the equivalent of the icy bathroom. The euphemism ruled. As if 'period' was not evasive enough, my mother described her monthly bleeding, and eventually mine, as 'being unwell'. It was not at all surprising to have to spend several days a month on a sofa, suffering, though why, and from what exactly, remained a mystery to me until I was twelve. She warned me when I was eleven that when I 'became a woman' she might have to slap my face because of the shock I would receive one day in the bathroom. Blood wasn't mentioned. The worst thing I and my classmates could imagine was someone – a boy especially, but even another girl, oh, anyone – seeing a sanitary towel hidden in our schoolbag. And the terror of 'coming on' and finding you had been walking around with a spot of blood on the back of your skirt… The shame was that people would know you were doing what every woman does once a month for a third of her life – bleeding.

At thirteen I came across an item in a home medical encyclopedia about 'self-abuse'. Though it suggested quite liberally that there was nothing dangerous about it, the name itself, and the fact that it had an entry, made it clear that it was a medical problem. It described 'touching the private parts', and I realised that I did that every night, drifting off to sleep, curled up in bed with my hand between my legs, holding my vulva. I had not the slightest notion of orgasm, nor did the article talk about the purpose of the touching, only that it was nothing to worry about, though it was a good idea to talk about it to a doctor if you did it regularly. I had my first sexual terror. Later, I would be regularly consumed with worry that I might be pregnant or have a venereal disease, but this was my first sexual bodily alarm (as it happened I didn't faint with fright on getting my period, though I wondered, when I told my mother, whether I shouldn't slap her shocked face). I was consumed by uncertainty, that cloud of sexual unknowing that hovered over our heads, fearing something was wrong with me, though I couldn't work out from the encyclopedia what exactly it was and what the consequences would be. Being fearful, vaguely guilty and feeling alone was what burgeoning sexuality meant to large numbers of people in the late Fifties and early Sixties.

In America the Beats, along with Humbert and his nymphet, were shocking readers and still getting banned for sexual explicitness, but in England we fell on *Lady Chatterley* in 1961, when it was finally published in an accessible paperback edition after a notorious court case ('Would you want your wives and servants reading this book?' the prosecuting counsel asked the jury). We were searching for information, though we got very little. Sexuality was there in the pages of books, but diffuse, metaphorised out of existence. Metaphor is little better than euphemism to information-hungry adolescents. Somerset Maugham and Neville Shute wrote what were thought to be steamy novels, but they were steamy in the same way that a bathroom mirror is steamy – you fail to see what you are looking at. I read them all hopefully, but only found my misty surmises effloresced into jungles of confusion. Yes, wellings and rushings and pumpings, and never-before-experienced experiences, but *what had actually happened*, what did they *do* and *how*? It was only when social class became a serious subject in novels, plays and films that sexual and many other silences were released into the wild. *Room at the Top* came out in 1957, and *Saturday Night and Sunday Morning* in 1960, *A Taste of Honey* and *The L-Shaped Room* in 1961 and '62. They began to clear the mist away, and linked a vivid sexuality to youth, education and social anger, though mostly for men. The women still longed, loved and feared that they'd get knocked up, and weren't so much sexually vivid as socially timorous or occasionally brave.

However, by the late Sixties, although we may not have done recreational drugs, we did do casual sex. We tried hard to make sex as casual as sleeping. There were, of course, couples. Two individuals bound together for longer or shorter periods, madly in love, or loving friends, or one of them having their heart broken by an unfaithful other, being betrayed or betraying in the old-fashioned way that casual sex didn't permit. But they were anomalies, we supposed, or were discovered to be people who had minded all along about things that we were supposed to have stopped caring about. People had sex because they and it were there, like climbing mountains but with less effort and preparation required, and, as we thought then, danger-free. It was late, someone would stay over or not go back to their own room. You might even really fancy someone, suddenly, or you'd think: why not? There never seemed to be a legitimate answer to that. It was on the one hand part of the vital and present task of experiencing experience, and on the other a contemporary version of good manners. Sex was a way of being polite to those who suggested it or who got into your bed. It was very difficult not to fuck someone who wanted to fuck you without feeling you were being very rude. My guess, no, my certainty, is that large numbers of people slept with friends, acquaintances and strangers that they had no desire for. I also guess that this was more desultory for women, few of whom, I regret to say, seemed as jaunty the following day as the men who waved them a cheery farewell. Part of the newness of the world we were creating was the abolition of jealousy, and the idea of possessing other people. The 'that's your problem' catch-all for complaints applied to sexual relations, too. You took responsibility for yourself and this meant not making demands on others whose wishes were different from your own. Clearly, this was not an equally balanced provision. Wanting overrode not wanting. To stop someone having something they wanted was to be a drag, really controlling, just laying 'your problem' on others who were unburdened by your hang-ups. But I do recall a few gentle souls who wandered into my room and asked tentatively, 'Want a fuck?' and then wandered out again without stopping to debate my problem if I replied with a sleepy, 'No, thanks.'

But there was a large principle at state. If sex was no longer going to be a taboo then it was hard to think of a good reason not to have it with anyone who came along. It was uncool to say no. It was easier to say yes than to explain. It was difficult to come up with a justification for refusing to have sex with someone that didn't seem selfish. The idea that rape was having sex with someone who didn't want to do it didn't apply very much in the late Sixties. On the basis that no means no, I was raped several times by men who arrived in my bed and wouldn't take no for an answer. But not wanting wasn't the main thing. It doesn't sound so exciting, this sexual revolution, does it? Mostly it wasn't. Open relationships were frequently tried, but I never came across any where at least one of the pair was not suffering and eventually unable to suppress it. There was a commune set up near my place which a friend of mine stayed in when he needed somewhere to live. The rules of the commune were that you weren't allowed to sleep with the same person for more than three nights in a row, so that no couples developed. Sex was free, relationships were forbidden. In order for the non-possessive rule to work, everyone there had to be prepared to sleep with everyone else – though I believe that men were exempted from having to have sex with men if they didn't want to. My friend found it very tiring packing up his bag and moving on to the next room every few days, and turned up at my flat from time to time to get a few regular nights' sleep.

In order to fight against the arbitrary moral codes the bourgeois world imposed on the young, the young imposed on themselves arbitrary physical requirements that took very little account of the complexity of human emotional connections. We cut a swathe through the conventions, but invented new conventions that gave us just as much heartache. Liberation, at least in its sexual form, was a new form of imposed morality, quite as restricting and causing at least as much repression as we accused our parents' generation of creating. Our elders called it permissiveness, but the permission we gave ourselves was more like a set of orders for disobeying our elders.

The journalist John Lloyd describes his experience of a commune, which sounds remarkably similar to the very one my friend had occasionally to escape from.

> In our flat, which we ran as a commune, the whole sex thing was extremely earnest. There was a lot of promiscuity, everybody had to swap partners. We didn't get into homosexuality, it was all heterosexuality. I'm not sure whether we really did elevate it above wife-swapping. It was quite exploitative of male and female. It was a lot of men liking to fuck a lot and saying to women, 'Why won't

you fuck me?' I remember saying that quite a lot. And some women who were strong and sensible enough said, 'Because I don't want to,' but quite often it was 'Well… all right…' Contraception was generally available, and there was an ethos of doing it, and it was good and it was liberating and it was an act of friendship or love. But we weren't really liberated – all of us had a lot of hang-ups. We had been brought up traditionally, even strictly, and to try to leap out of your own habits and upbringing into this blissful state where there were not hang-ups was of course interesting psychologically, but it was completely impossible. And all the jealousies and tensions just grew exponentially.[5]

Another version is Richard Neville's afterthought:

Part of battling against a joyless morality – don't fuck until you get married, and when you do you'll both be so dreadful you'll probably get divorced. I had come from a very bad marriage and I was interested in men and women working out a different sort of sexual/social behaviour. But of course there is some truth in the idea that this was institutionalising getting laid, providing a political framework for sex. I loved women and I loved making love to them. I loved fucking and there were lots of people around who felt the same. I don't think that anyone was pushed into bed by me. A lot of girls climbed through my window.[6]

Communes weren't a brand new idea, but we could hardly avoid investigating them. The nuclear family model was beginning to look very limited. So we set up communes or lived communally in our flats, sharing the washing-up and each other's lovers, and then discovered what that meant in the actual day-to-day living. Usually a terrible mess and a lot of anger – regarding both the washing-up and the sex. The communal dream invariably ended in acrimony as all the tensions of the old way of living pulled the group idea apart. Children, love, money, work, privacy and ownership were all ancient and crucial issues that for the most part we failed successfully to negotiate. To tell each other that other cultures lived in this way didn't take into account our lack of experience in living in any way at all. All the time, in every aspect of our lives, the thing we forgot, and the thing that enabled us to do what we did, was the fact of our being young.

~

And once again, as with the funding for our radical ways of life, it wasn't the young really who were in charge of enabling this sexual revolution that our elders and ourselves talked so much about. The pill, the great enabler of fearless sex (for a short while) was developed by that older generation. And the easing of sexual repression in the UK began, if it had a beginning, in the heart of everything we most despised: government. Roy Jenkins was Home Secretary of the Labour government between 1965 and 1967. Born in 1920, he was not part of the Sixties generation but an upper-middle-class liberal with no time for Victorian morality. In 1959 he wrote a pamphlet called *Is Britain Civilised?*

The need is to campaign for a general climate of opinion favourable to gaiety and tolerance, and opposed to puritanical restriction and a drab, ugly pattern of life. It is not really a job for politicians, of course, although they, like any other leaders of opinion, can do something to set the tone...But the important thing is to encourage them all, and to recognise that one form of intolerance breeds another and one type of drabness makes another more likely. Let us be on the side of those who want people to be free to live their own lives, to make their own mistakes, and to decide in an adult way and provided they do not infringe the rights of others, the code by which they wish to live; and on the side too of experiment and brightness, of better buildings and better food, of better music (jazz as well as Bach) and better books, of fuller lives and greater freedom. In the long run these things will be more important than even the most perfect of economic policies.[7]

The permission was already available, long before the Sixties generation were blamed for instigating the permissive society. During his time as Home Secretary, Jenkins (hardly a radical socialist) oversaw the relaxation of a series of legal curbs on sexual and social freedom: on divorce, the abolition of theatre censorship, the legalisation of abortion and the decriminalisation of homosexuality. The world wasn't waiting for the post-war children to make it free, the post-war children were reinventing their own freedom in a climate made ready for them. Jenkins's near contemporary Mary Whitehouse, a woman who described herself as an 'ordinary housewife' and was in the vanguard of the backlash against all things permissive, complained about the terrible freedoms the young were taking, but she complained much more about the liberality of those like the Home Secretary, the BBC's director-general Hugh Carlton Greene, and the Bishop of Woolwich. All of them, as far as we were concerned, were the establishment, the grown-ups, those whom we gave ourselves permission to rebel against.

Nevertheless, it was in the late Sixties that the Gay Liberation Movement took off. In London, mysterious graffiti appeared on walls everywhere saying simply ''Tis Gay'. To this day, I don't know if it was part of a campaign or just some happy wall-writer extolling the joys of life. It was certainly my first sighting of the word 'gay' to mean homosexual – if indeed that's what it was. It was much clearer in Greenwich Village, New York, when on 29 June 1969 the police raided the Stonewall Inn one time too many, and the gays, drag queens and transgendered patrons finally had enough. The Stonewall riots lasted for days, with local people swelling the rebellion, blockading the street and torching the inn while the drag queens sang their anthem:

> We are the Stonewall Girls
> We wear our hair in curls
> We wear no underwear
> We show our pubic hair
> We wear our dungarees
> Above our nelly knees

Gay Power was born in the Sixties to battle alongside

other persecuted groups – blacks, Hispanics and women – who were fighting for justice. If the general sexual revolution had its problems, gay power was the acceleration of a genuine liberation. Not that homophobia has been decisively defeated, any more than racism or sexism, even now, but attitudes have been changed, and even if it only means that bigots have to whisper their bigotry to each other, it is a real achievement of which (along with those engaged in the battle previously) the Sixties generation can be proud.

4

REMAKING THE WORLD

...the advance guard of the new order. We wished to transform Western civilisation because we regarded it as politically, morally and culturally bankrupt. That was the hallmark of 1968.

Tariq Ali, *Street Fighting Years*, 1987

There was an American staying in our flat in Covent Garden, on the run from the US draft to Vietnam. Seymour was a small, dark, quite round, full-bearded, long-haired, gentle soul, softly spoken, who sat in the lotus position and smiled benignly at the world he looked out at when he was tripping and even when he wasn't. We were pals. We might have had sex once or twice, I can't remember, but it wasn't the point. On Sunday morning, 17 March 1968, we set off together to Trafalgar Square for the start of the second Grosvenor Square anti-Vietnam war demonstration. He had more urgent reasons than me for protesting the Vietnam war but I'd been marching and sitting down, not being moved (actually being both physically and emotionally moved) since the Aldermaston march in 1963, when I was still just fifteen. Back then I remember walking in the middle of a great straggling column of people, mostly older than me, but many not very much older, who were chanting, singing, debating politics, and feeling I was part of something undeniably

important – the continuing existence of the planet, actually – thrilled to be among them, at last, to have found a
group I liked appearing to belong with. The gaiety was
powerful and beguiling, the uniform of denim, long
hair and beards reassuring. We were the beatniks and
weirdies the popular press wrote about and our parents
worried so much about. I was marching with a group of
people in their late twenties, who met regularly at the
Highlander and the French pubs in Dean Street, and
the Partisan café round the corner, where the New Left
congregated. One of them was the son of a friend of the
woman I was staying with, and they had been charged
with my care.

It was a moment when I felt I might be in the right
place, among these like-minded, humanist, socialist,
hard-drinking, fast-talking, clever people who treated
me not as if they were looking after me but as one of their
group. But there were moments, as I put one foot in front
of another through the towns of Reading and Slough,
when the point of what we were doing vividly came back
to me. I really did believe that sooner or later the bombs
would explode in Washington and Moscow, Paris and
London. I was quite sure that I would have to live part of
my life, perhaps most of my life, in a post-nuclear devas-
tated world. If I lived at all. I knew it in the way that children suddenly come to know that one day inescapably
they will die, and try to understand it by rehearsing the
catastrophe as they lie in bed at night, while their parents
believe they are dreaming fairy tales. Much of the time,

of course, like the children, I forgot, and behaved like a young person with their whole life in front of them, but that knowing place would intermittently reassert itself, making me almost dizzy with the fact of it. So I looked around sometimes during the three-day march at all of us having such a good time, comrades, conversationalists, drinking pals, and flirting the promise of all kind of pleasures to come, while nonetheless feeling fervently opposed to a politics based on mortal fear, and I wondered if everyone really believed that the worst would actually happen, in the way I did in those moments of certainty. Perhaps everyone thinks that they are the only ones who believe the worst. Or perhaps all fifteen-year-olds think they are the only ones who really know the truth. Anyway, I couldn't quite imagine that my companions and the other thousands on the march, some of them quite militant for those early days, truly believed they were going to go up in or die slowly from the forthcoming planetary explosion.

What went with that feeling of being sole keeper of the truth was astonishment, a complete inability to comprehend how those who were in charge of the world could operate as they did. Not just their building of nuclear weapons, and the creation of fear, but their acceptance of, let alone their complicity in the interrelated wickednesses of social and educational inequality, racism and poverty. I had the flashing sense that it was a kind of dream world I inhabited, that I would wake up and, *of course*, none of those unthinkable ills were permitted by rational, educated, responsible people. I knew a little about the required intricacies and compromises of *realpolitik*, inasmuch as I'd studied European history for A level, but what was more *real* than the fact of hungry, sick and dispossessed human beings living on the same planet as the well-fed, highly schooled and skilled people in charge who could do something about it? I was not, to put it another way, political. I paid attention to the world and saw suffering being tolerated for political and economic reasons, or greed, or laziness, and, being somewhat new on the planet, it shocked me.

Five years later, I hadn't grown any more sophisticated. The American invasion of Vietnam wasn't a British war, not even a blunder of the British empire, but the Wilson government publicly supported the Americans, though it did manage to avoid – that time – sending troops as proof of their support. But at that point in the history of the world, as ever since, it mattered very little what the British government did or didn't do. What the Americans were doing in Vietnam was startlingly clear; everywhere people watched TV reports and read in newspapers of a world power napalming peasant villages in the hunt for an ill-equipped guerrilla army, in the name of US security. We learned of American soldiers turning savage against the 'gooks' – the less than human, the not-us – and transforming ancient South Vietnamese cities into whorehouses for their rest and recreation. It was shown around the world, for everyone to see. No one I knew, apart from the draft-dodging Seymour, was caught up in the war, but that wasn't the point. Something was different from previous wars and foreign adventures: access by the media and to the media, and for me and many others of the post-war generation, the world could no longer be divided up into those I knew and those I didn't. What happened far away to strangers mattered. If what America did wasn't my fault, I had no doubt that it was my responsibility to stand against it.

Tariq Ali, unlike me, *was* political, but he too was young. Speaking to the Vietnamese contingent from the National Liberation Front at the Helsinki Peace Conference in 1965 had convinced him 'that there was one overriding priority for radicals, socialists and democrats in the West. We had to do everything in our power – if necessary turn the world upside down – to help the Vietnamese drive the Americans out of their country. I had thrown myself wholeheartedly into political activities related to the Vietnam war on my return to Britain.'[8] He became the visible head of the British Vietnam Solidarity Campaign, which had organised the first, and now the much-anticipated second anti-war march on the US embassy in Grosvenor Square.

~

The sweet-natured Seymour underwent an astonishing seachange as we arrived in Trafalgar Square for the speeches and the beginning of the march. Clutching my hand and dragging me behind him (I think now of Alice being rushed by the Red Queen to the next square on the chessboard – 'Faster, faster!'), he manoeuvred through the crowd until he found the group he was looking for. It was widely reported that the German SDS, led by Rudi Dutschke, had come over for the march. The German students had organised the first European demonstration against the war and, along with the Japanese, led the field in militancy. Seymour, his dark beard and short stature now seeming not emblematic of peace and love but the very insignia of a feral street-fighting man, forced his way to the front line of the German contingent, taking me with him. I don't think he knew I was there any more, he just held onto my hand firmly because the tension and fury in him kept his grip firm. The SDS wore crash helmets and had with them a thick wooden stave which they held at waist height across the eleven or so strong young men (and me) as they lined up to begin the demonstration. We set off at a rapid marching pace. Soon someone shouted an order and the front line, including Seymour and me, stopped. We were not marching properly, Dutschke or whoever it was bellowed. That is, I wasn't. He glared in my direction. We were to march at a uniform pace. He spoke in German but his meaning was clear. We set off again, the leader counting us firmly into step. Left, right, left, right. I did my best, but I've always felt ridiculous trying to be synchronised – group dancing or singing, uniforms, any of that stuff makes me cringe. Every now and then at a barked signal the line broke suddenly into a real run, an organised trot, but still (apart from me) keeping in step. It was a small but quite alarming charge, an organised, running phalanx, which returned to a brisk march only at the next shout of our leader. I was hopeless. Not just unrehearsed but innately rubbish at doing anything in formation. I was used to the soft shuffle, the occasional moving jive to a jazz band of the Aldermaston march. The German group were very strict, and I got told off a lot. 'Keep in step! Stay in time!' It wasn't that I wanted to be there, but Seymour's iron grip wasn't loosening and no matter how hard I looked at him he kept his face to the front, and his eyes glazed in excitement.

Near Marble Arch there was an extraordinary manoeuvre. After one of the sudden charges, a police-man came and stood in front of us, holding us up with a warning not to do it again; we were to walk like everyone else. Without anyone saying anything, but perfectly in unison, the two ends of the front line moved ahead of the middle, bringing round those behind them, and in seconds the policeman had been surrounded, as if by an amoeba putting out pseudopodia to consume its food. The pincer swung open and then closed, the two ends meeting in a new middle, swallowing him completely, as the front line reformed in an orderly fashion, conceal-ing what was going on behind and in the middle of the group. Something was happening behind us, even as we marched, left, right, left, right. A scuffle, a digesting of the bacteria we had consumed, and, as if nothing had happened, we continued neatly and in time on our way. I looked back, but I was too short to see over the forest of helmets. I don't know what happened to the policeman. It was as if he was lost for ever.

When we got to the metal fence surrounding Grosvenor Square we were brought to a halt for a short conference. Then the whole group were given a shouted instruction to push back a few yards. On a signal, they began a full charge, complete with an almighty bellowing. They held out the wooden stave in front of them, straight-armed, and it and I hit the fence. They were strong, muscular young men, prepared for a fight, angry and flooded with adrenalin – their use of military formation and varying manoeuvres helped them with that. The hurtling force from the rows behind pressed hard on the front line, the boots and the stave given extra power to attack the barrier, and after two or three runs at it, during the last of which I, of course, fell over, the fence was flattened. Demonstrators poured into the Square through the breach, while I kept very still on the ground and hoped one of their great triumphant boots wouldn't snap my spine. Eventually, someone lifted me up. I'd lost Seymour, who had finally dropped my hand in the scrummage, and I last saw him running, head down and screaming like a dying bull, towards the front entrance of the Embassy, a small, dark invasion force of his own. The German contingent were all long gone, headed in the same direction, ready to confront the lines of police standing in rows with their arms linked, as if they were about to sing 'Auld Lang Syne', to protect the integrity of the Embassy. I stood still and caught my breath about halfway into the square. Then the horses arrived, galloping out of the streets at the sides of the Embassy, huge and terrifying and to me, pretty crazed by now, like a multiplication of the Four Horsemen, hooves thundering on the grass. The mounted police swung about with their batons, landing blows on heads, necks and shoulders, wherever and on whomever they fell. The crowd fought back, embattled and largely trapped in the square. Even experienced demonstrators in England were unused to this degree of not casual but joyful police violence. They caught at the batons, at legs and arms, and pulled some of the police from their mounts, while spreading the word that it was all right, the horses were trained not to trample people. I hoped they were right, it seemed like a lot of faith to put in a posse of large and frightened animals, but I was more worried about being trampled by the demonstrators who were being pressed back in a mass by the mounted police, and when I found myself eventually backed against a substantial tree it was perfectly plain to me that I was going to be crushed to death.

I wasn't. The crowd, smarter than I was, streamed to either side of the tree and I slipped away from it. I fled the fighting and the crowds and took myself home, shaken by the violence of the police and perhaps more by the military organisation of the demonstrators. I was also astonished and worried about Seymour, whom I'd seen for a moment in hand-to-hand combat outside the Embassy with a policeman who towered over him, while gentle Seymour threw his fists and feet at him furiously. But somehow he managed not to get arrested, and turned up at the flat scratched and bruised late that night, utterly different. Dark, bitter, brooding, furious. He stopped taking drugs and paced around the flat enraged as if he had been incarcerated after all. He was completely transformed. Either that, or the person he had been suppressing during his period of sweetness, his smiling and stoned exile, had at last been released. Within a couple of weeks Seymour decided to return to the States. There were ways of getting back incognito, he'd discovered. He proposed to live in hiding, wild in the woods, doing whatever he had to do to fight the US government. I had a grey cape that was really part of the uniform of the Greycoat School which I'd bought in a jumble sale. I gave it to him when he left to help him keep warm in the woods during his resistance. I never saw or heard from him again.

∼

There were other versions of changing the world. For readers of Marcuse, even such as Tariq Ali, for example:

> …the long march did not mean 'boring from within' but gaining experience of production, education, computers, mass media, the organisation of production, while simultaneously preserving one's own political consciousness. The aim of the long march was to build counter-institutions.[9]

This was a serious preparation for a new order, but I think there were very few young people prepared to forgo the more demonstrative, emotionally satisfying forms of revolution, or engage seriously if covertly with the 'straight' world in the way 'boring from within' (in both senses) required. There were endless meetings, of course, if you had signed up to the VSC (Vietnam Solidarity Campaign), IMG (International Marxist Group), IS (International Socialists) or WRP (Workers' Revolutionary Party); you could keep to agendas, take minutes, debate and make points of order, and feel you were part of the righteous few who were in possession of the true way. In this sense, too, I was not political. I continued to see and abhor what was wrong, but I wasn't convinced by any of the true and mutually exclusive solutions on offer. Other people's certainty always made me uncertain. I failed to join anything and merely continued my long-standing inclination for non-engagement. I told myself that smoking dope, dropping acid, shooting up Methedrine and reading about other ways of being was a form of resistance against the unsatisfactory world. I settled for outlawhood. Or escape, as others, more politically committed, would reasonably have said. It suited my temperament, and the interdisciplinary arguments and fractional in-fighting in the meetings I did attend – I made small efforts from time to time – seemed far too much like microcosmic versions of what went on in the real world that we all so much disliked. I had the airy idealism of M. Poupin,

Henry James's refugee from the Paris Commune in *The Princess Casamassima*:

> He was a Republican of the old-fashioned sort…
> humanitary and idealistic, infinitely addicted to fraternity
> and equality, and inexhaustibly surprised and exasperated
> at finding so little enthusiasm for them in the land of his
> exile…he believed that the day was to come when all the
> nations of the earth would abolish their frontiers and
> armies and custom-houses, and embrace on both cheeks,
> and cover the globe with boulevards…where the human
> family would sit, in groups, at little tables according to
> affinities, drinking coffee…and listening to the music of
> the spheres.[10]

But even M. Poupin turned out to be more politically active than I was. I was uneasily aware, also, how very different the European resentment of the establishment was from the American resistance against the Vietnam war. For both that war was the core issue, the gravest and most pressing injustice, but my experience with Seymour before and after the Grosvenor Square demonstration made it clear that we post-war Europeans were waging a more theoretical battle than Americans who refused call-up or returned mentally or physically shattered, or who watched their children disappear into the South East Asian morass the United States government had got itself into. Britain, as far as I was concerned, was now a backwater (what Gore Vidal once called one of the 'lands' – Iceland, Newfoundland, Greenland), and all the better for it, it seemed to me. While on the one hand, any injustice was my and everyone's concern wherever it might happen, and we were right to support the opposition in the US and Vietnam, it was in the places where the young were being drafted, where students (in Kent State) were being shot and killed for demonstrating, and in the underground tunnels of Vietnam itself, that the serious business of world-changing was going on. For the life of me I looked and couldn't believe that the British Left could have more than a mildly irritant effect on those who made the world go on as it ever did.

Nonetheless, I had a kind of hope. I think many people did. One day, I supposed, our lot would be in charge and then things would be different. It didn't cross my mind then that 'our lot' would not remain our lot, or that there were another lot (and far more of them) in our generation who were as pragmatic about power as the unreconstructed generations before us. Like the young at all times, I imagined that such as us had never happened before, and that nothing was ever going to be the same again once the old had passed into their pottering retirement. What the young don't get is that *they are young*; the old are right, young is a phase the old go through. It's just as well, I suppose, that the young don't see it that clearly. Best to leave disappointment for later.

Actually, in line with Vidal's view of our island, anyone in backwater Britain who wasn't prepared to travel at short notice was likely to miss the serious battles that were going on in the world – even those quite nearby. In 1968, it looked to those of us peering through the sweetshop window of the English Channel as if the world was catching fire. In Prague, Dubcek was proceeding towards M. Poupin's more 'humanitary' socialism, until the Soviet tanks steamrollered him into submission to the party line in August. In France, for decades a seriously politically active nation, there were a few days in May when the socialist dream looked like breaking into real life, as the unions joined dissenting students and came out in protest on the streets against de Gaulle's government. The regular citizens of Paris opened their doors and offered sanctuary to the rebels against the fearsome CRS (Compagnies Républicaines de Sécurité) riot police. Cobbles were ripped out of the ground, cars upturned, barricades were built, running battles with the CRS closed the Latin Quarter to all but revolutionary sympathisers, and the Sorbonne was taken by the demonstrators who held great political and philosophical debates. From our side of *La Manche* it looked astonishing, a reality, as radical politics had never seemed in England, and quite not-undoable – but then even before most of the British radicals could catch the train to the Gare du Nord, it was over. De Gaulle had done a deal, made threats and promises, and with incomprehensible suddenness, the fire died. The revolution was over with no more result than a few missing cobbles on the streets. It was unfathomable, this dying away of the revolution-in-progress. In Italy the Red Brigade and in Germany the Baader-Meinhof gang were taking guerrilla action against individuals, and at the very end of the period, in

1974, in San Francisco, the Symbionese Liberation Army snatched heiress Patty Hearst and turned her into a gun-toting revolutionary while demanding that the Hearst family deliver $6 million of food in trucks to be distributed on the streets in the Bay Area.

But in the UK it was mostly back to theory, after a little argy-bargy at the London School of Economics – a battle over the destruction of the iron gates – and a take-over of the University of London Students' Union swimming pool in Malet Street. In 1963 I really did believe that the world would go up in a nuclear conflagration; by the end of 1968, I still thought so, but if the revolution hadn't taken where it had been serious – in serious Europe and serious America and in very serious Latin America, where the previous year Che Guevara had been killed – what chance was there for it in England, where the students were universally regarded as long-haired layabouts, where civil servants never turned a hair, so sure were they of the reliable conservatism of the generality of the people, and the workers marched in favour of Enoch Powell's racist call for an end to immigration before the Thames turned to a river of blood? The flame still flickered hopefully in those meetings where varieties of Trotskyist, Marxist-Leninist or Maoist comrades maintained their faith in the eventual inevitable revolutionary outcome, but I couldn't convince myself.

~

The obscenity trial against *Oz* magazine in June 1971, for producing their Schoolkids issue, written and drawn by school-age adolescents, was a marker of the end of British dissidence – a marker, too, of the tone and seriousness of British dissidence. The teenage Vivian Berger's energetic and priapic Rupert Bear sitting astride an upturned Gipsy Granny was too much for the decent morals of Inspector Luff of the Yard. The three defendants (Richard Neville, Jim Anderson and Felix Dennis) chirpily showed up at court in short trousers and gymslips to show their contempt, but when, even before they were found guilty, and they were held without bail, their long hair was viciously (and illegally) cut short, it should have been a warning that the permissive times were coming to a close and that the grown-ups were out of patience. It was beginning to look as if it wasn't us who had given ourselves permission, but Them. And the permission was being withdrawn. There were some braver interpretations. From Germaine Greer, for example:

> At last they've stopped laughing at us, which means we can go back to laughing at them. We can be illegal. We can conspire. We can come closer together again as the space around us closes. There are more of us now, but that's nothing compared to how many of us there'll be tomorrow. Eradication means plucking up by the roots – but our roots are where they'll never get at, they're sunk down somewhere inside of every family in the British Isles.[11]

This was bold and hopeful, but hopeless. The forces of

morality – Mary Whitehouse's various clean-up organisations, the Festival of Light supported by Lord Long-
ford, DJ Jimmy Savile and pop singer Cliff Richard –
called for a Nationwide Petition for Public Decency, and
campaigned for 'traditional values' to prevail by virtue
of the moral majority coming out to be counted, against
drugs, sexual and especially gay liberation, and what
they called obscenity (which Mary Whitehouse called
'filth'), wherever it was to be found. Like Germaine Greer,
they also believed that they represented every family in
the British Isles, and probably with more justification.
Though in their separate categories sex (clandestine and
in the dark), drugs (cigarettes, alcohol) and even some
rock 'n' roll (that'll be Cliff again) were popular activities
in most families in the British Isles, the more dangerous
youth-packaged version *Sex-and-Drugs-and-Rock'n Roll*,
incorporating radical politics and alternative lifestyles,
was always only a minority way of life. Except for clan
meetings on demonstrations and music festivals, we
kept ourselves mostly to ourselves (and only ever joked
about spiking the water system with LSD) and hoped not
to be among those whom society chose now and again
to make an example of, like the *Oz* threesome, Mick
Jagger[12] (*The Times*' Leader's butterfly broken on a wheel)
and numbers of unnamed people who went to prison for
years for possession of any quantity of hashish.

So it was a bit of a surprise when bombs exploded
from 1968 onwards, at the homes of various politicians,
on the threshold of Biba, under a BBC outside broadcast

van at the Miss World competition in 1970, as well as a hundred and more other places. Various anarchist groups had promised havoc from time to time, but it being England, neither the establishment, the regular Far Left or the counter-cultural types expected much actually to happen. Some of the bombs came with communiqués announcing retributive justice by armed working-class revolutionaries, signed sometimes by 'The Angry Brigade'. Finally, eight students were arrested, four of them in a house where the police found a children's John Bull printing kit with the words 'Angry Brigade' set up. It was enough, with some dubious forensics, to convict four of them, who were sentenced to ten years in prison. Bombs still went off while the defendants were in custody, and it seems clear that 'The Angry Brigade' was more of a brand name than a specific group of the eight people imprisoned, none of whom was convicted of actually causing explosions. But the press rejoiced that the unpleasant business of the Sixties was now being cleared up, though there wasn't long to wait before the IRA brought to the British mainland some unpleasant business of their own. The Angry Brigade was as far as Britain got in the Sixties towards *serious* resistance, even if it was by no means as organised as the triumphant forces of law and order wanted the country to believe.

The admirable David Widgery, lifelong member of International Socialism that he remained, later observed wryly of the radical Sixties:

There was a general re-discovery of the Russian
Revolution and of the various oppositional tendencies
in the Soviet 1920s, and a tendency to chuck lumps of
Trotsky and the young Marx in with some Reich. At
its best it seemed like a gathering of post-electronic
Renaissance people, passionately serious but intoxicated
by LSD as well as alcohol and exponents of social theory
instead of sword fighting.[13]

The division between the Underground and the Far Left
was sharper than this suggests. The underground press,
IT (*International Times*), *Oz* and *Ink*, certainly reported
the street fighting, and gave space to some of the theorists
of the Left, but usually in a wild variety of overprinted
colours and optically challenging patterns, which made
it very hard to read if you weren't actually tripping. They
imposed psychedelia over the assumed dullness of Marxist-Leninist theory, giving their readers something pretty
to look at without having to bother struggling through
the prose. The counter-culture's credo was rather different from the strict discipline of the comrades:

It is living by what you believe, with a set of attitudes
shared by, but not sacred to, a number of people intent
on challenging their society to live up to its promise...
It is a movement of social liberation through individual
liberation. Everyone must be free to do their own thing.
The Underground puts self at the centre of its spectrum.
That is, no form of social or political liberation, however
desirable, can take place unless its first priority is to allow
each individual to determine his own desires, free from
psychological, political or conventional pressures.[14]

Like the forthcoming socialist paradise I had trouble believing in, this too required more faith than I was able to summon. It was very clear, just from living communally in the Covent Garden flat, that being free to do one's own thing became highly problematical when one's own thing clashed with someone else's thing. Compromise was quite against the spirit of the times and in any case a nonsense where the self was central. When someone else's freedom seemed inimical to your own, the phrase 'that's your problem' immediately reappeared.

In the Sixties we were reading all kinds of texts which dealt in large-scale, complete theories, but the actual living experience was altogether more messy and fractured. It ought to have been immediately obvious that liberation and libertarianism were not at all one and the same thing. To be liberated enough to put yourself at the centre of the spectrum and to determine your own desires without reference to 'psychological, political or conventional pressures' should have made one helpless with laughter. But it seemed, at first, to make complete sense. Or at least to be seductive enough to allow our intellects to slip away from examining the words very thoroughly. One crucial truth about the Sixties is that the difference between Buckman's set of beliefs and those of Conservative government of the Eighties was, in practice, very much slighter than we imagined. We wailed during the Thatcher era: 'No, no, that wasn't what we meant, at all.' She was anathema to us, the very opposite of what we had hoped for the future, but perhaps our own careless thinking gave the radical individualism of her government at least a rhetorical foothold. Her founding statement that 'There is no such thing as society' could easily be derived from the 'self at the centre' that seemed to many of us in the Sixties so unproblematical. We do have some responsibility there, I think, but Widgery was not merely indulging in the nostalgia of defeat when he refused to reject the values of the politically active Sixties, even if, in a way, his words have a final ring of the inescapable self-centredness which may be all that the Sixties generation are left with:

> And despite the manifest lack of success in the larger tasks we have set ourselves, I persist in regarding the commitment I acquired in 1968 as the most fruitful and rewarding of my adult life.[15]

There were, of course, those, the great majority, doubtless, who, having finished with their wild youth, put on proper suits come the mid-Seventies and went off to work and a regular life, becoming all their parents could have wished, having just gone through a phase, as the more liberal of the grown-ups had always suggested. But some – these days called, derogatorily, idealists – maintained their former sense that 'society' exists, and believe it persists, even beyond the strident years of Margaret Thatcher and the officially approved decades of self-interest and greed that have followed. We are the disappointed remnant, the rump of the Sixties.

~

As to the liberation of women – there's no doubt that, like gay liberation, the second wave of twentieth-century feminism, which had barely got under way by 1970, has had, and continues to have, a powerful influence. Certainly, most women who lived through the early and late Sixties whether as political molls or psychedelic chicks can recall that they were mostly of ornamental, sexual, domestic or secretarial value to the men striking out for radical shores. The Left was never known for its willingness to embrace gender equality, but no more were the 'heads' or the entrepreneurs of the counter-culture. In a relatively public way, in relatively specific parts of the world, things have changed for women. Domestic violence is more seriously policed, rape is usually taken to be a major crime, and I would no longer (as I was in 1970) be asked for a (non-existent) husband's signature when I applied as a single woman to have the gas service turned on in my new flat. But like racial equality, women's liberation is honoured in legislation more than in the private attitudes of many individuals. Even in the wealthy West women's pay is on average substantially less than that of men doing equivalent work, and the difficulties and expense of childcare often mean that women are going out to work to pay for childcare in order to work. I don't think that personal inclinations and opinions in general have changed very much in the vast majority of either the developing or the developed world. Get just a little beyond the educated middle-class enclaves – read red-top newspapers, listen to men talk in bars – and the heart sinks. Young women themselves, not all, of course, consider feminism nothing to do with them. A student standing for office at Newnham College, Cambridge (one of the two last all-women colleges in the University) recently felt able to stand on the platform of *not* being a feminist. To a Sixties observer, these days the liberation of women on a Saturday night in town looks very like the freedom to get falling-down drunk. Perhaps it isn't for earlier liberationists to have an opinion on what *kind* of equality women who now can choose should take – it may be just as impertinent as Western nations decreeing that only their kind of democracy is acceptable for 'liberated' dictatorships. Women are, of course, much freer than they were in the Fifties, when to be married with children often meant being trapped for life without the possibility of an independent income. But I'm not sure that there aren't many women who are in a similar position today. A woman in her mid-sixties (just a few years older than me) told me recently that the problem with retirement was that now she had to think about what her husband was going to have for lunch every day, as well as what to buy for dinner. She meant her husband's retirement from the bank. She had brought up the children and kept the fridge stocked. The Sixties, as I knew them, had entirely passed her by.

It started much earlier, and, as nearly everything does, in the US. Betty Friedan published *The Feminine Mystique* in 1963 and founded NOW (the National Organization of Women). In the UK, Sheila Rowbotham wrote an article in 1968 that began, 'The first question is why do we stand for it?' in the *New Left Review*, and as part of the editorial collective persuaded *Black Dwarf* to follow 1968's 'Year of the Heroic Guerrilla' with 1969's 'Year of the Militant Woman'. It wasn't until October 1970 that Germaine Greer's *The Female Eunuch* came out, but by then there were already numbers of women's consciousness-raising groups, talking about the limitations of their lives, the need to find fulfilling work outside childcare, equal pay, their experience of men's contempt and chauvinism, discussing the nature of the female orgasm and helping each other with mirrors to take a first peek at the anatomy of their vaginas (something men had always been doing). No one then thought that a woman prime minister would be in Downing Street within ten years. No one then thought that if such a miraculous event could ever happen in a country where women weren't even allowed to read the news on television for fear of trivialising it, the situation of women (along with everyone else not grasping at personal gain) would get worse. In the light of the resistance to women's liberation in the Sixties (Black Power leader Stokely Carmichael famously declared when asked the position of women that it was 'on their backs'), it isn't altogether surprising that militant absurdities occurred such as the Sisterwrite Bookshop refusing to let the two-year-old son of a woman just arrived in London into the café with his mother. I watched as she protested, 'But I can't leave him alone in the middle of Upper Street, and I want to look at the noticeboard,' and received a welcoming smile to her but no easing of the anti-male rule. There were theoreticians and practitioners of lesbian S&M, girl-child-only crèches at women's discos, and a feminist zoologist in Scandinavia who proposed a change of name for the orang-utan – which means in Malay 'Man of the Forest' – to the Malay for 'Person of the Forest'. But it was difficult to laugh too much at the logical-conclusionists – say anything in the early Seventies about the rights of women or men's patronising attitudes, and there was an instant accusation that you would be one of those women's libber, bra-burning, unshaven lesbian girls. And aside from the Separatists there were women who worked in unions and lobbied government for equal pay legislation, for child-care assistance, who men had to listen to explaining to them what was wrong with even their liberal views of women's rights. Right into the 1980s, when my ex picked up our daughter from school two or three times a week, I was told by other mothers when I was in the playground waiting for her how fortunate I was to have such a marvellous man.

~

Forty years on there has been no remission in war and civil strife, no lessening of hunger in underdeveloped parts of the world. The Berlin Wall came down and the

Velvet Revolution occurred in Prague in 1989 and the Russian empire collapsed. I watched it happening on television, as people from East Berlin dumped their undesirable Trabant cars and headed west to trade up, they believed, to BMWs. The first free election happened in South Africa in 1994 to the astonished delight of those who had been active against the apartheid regime for decades, but fifteen years on the wealth is still largely in the hands of whites and multinational companies, the townships remain, people are grumbling that the blacks are suffering from a 'culture of resentment' that is causing the South African economy to collapse. Wherever you look, over the past forty years, nationalism and capitalism have triumphed. The Russians developed an instant mafia to replace the Communist Party elites, and as I write, the current president of Russia has moved troops into Georgia and is talking about a new Cold War. Nothing has changed in the politics of the West, and the newly developing countries are clamouring to repeat the phantasm of 'progress' in spite of the likelihood that the planet is only a decade or two away from environmental collapse. It is almost astonishing how little has changed, except in the realm of technology. We have more toys to play with while big business and governments are almost indistinguishable ('We are intensely relaxed about people getting filthy rich,' said Peter Mandelson, speaking for New Labour in 1998), and vie with each other only to keep taxes down. For a decade so notorious for its politically radical youth, it's quite remarkable how little effect we had.

There have, of course, been changes, politically and socially, some of them legislative, but I don't think they have penetrated into the assumptions of the great majority of the human race. I can't feel as positive even as David Widgery's limited optimism about the long-term effect of the radicalism of the Sixties:

> We changed attitudes but not structure. We succeeded in changing attitudes profoundly but did not have the strength to change the economic and therefore political power structure fundamentally.[16]

5

PROJECTING THE FUTURE

School teaches us that instruction produces learning. The existence of schools produces the demand for schooling. Once we have learned to need school, all our activities tend to take the shape of client relationships to other specialized institutions. Once the self-taught man or woman has been discredited, all nonprofessional activity is rendered suspect. In school we are taught that valuable learning is the result of attendance; that the value of learning increases with the amount of input; and, finally, that this value can be measured and documented by grades and certificates. In fact, learning is the human activity which least needs manipulation by others. Most learning is not the result of instruction. It is rather the result of unhampered participation in a meaningful setting.

Ivan Illich, *Deschooling Society*, 1971

We started South Villas Comprehensive – later to be Freightliners Free School – in 1971 with eight pupils, seven from the same family, two teachers and the promise of $100. It was thought up on a Friday and opened for business in my two-roomed flat in North London the following Monday. It was an entirely pragmatic invention. An intervention. That Friday afternoon a woman knocked on my door. She introduced herself as the social worker of some local kids I had got to know who hung out in the streets and adventure playground nearby.

'Allie B. says you're training to be a teacher and that you're interested in alternative education. The thing is that all the B. children are going to be split up and taken into care next week, for persistent truanting. Allie said you talked to her about free schools. If you started one for them I might be able to keep them out of local authority care and make a case for them to stay at home and together. But it needs to be up and running with a timetable and syllabus and something on paper by Monday, so I can show it to the case conference and get them to put the care order on hold.'

In 1971, the dog days of the Sixties, it didn't seem impossible to start a school over a weekend. I was training to be a teacher and I had just had an article published (my first) in a radical magazine called *Children's Rights* about a teaching practice I'd done. I phoned Roger, the editor, and asked if he had any ideas. Energy was the thing. I never had much, but Roger was full of it. By Saturday afternoon we had promises from local people to teach weekly or twice-weekly sessions. We produced a timetable, with lessons on architecture by a local architect who would also double up as a maths teacher; art and pottery were promised from a nearby artist who knew a potter who had a studio. Woodwork was taken care of by a carpenter who had a workshop a few streets away. French would be taught by a local woman at home with small children. A dropout physics graduate we knew would do science and I would take care of English. Roger, with a degree in politics and history, would teach history and current affairs and there was a swimming pool close by for PE. A friend in California offered us 100 dollars a month to keep us going with outings, equipment and lunches while we sorted out funding, and my flat was available, as was the virtually derelict basement of the family council house the kids lived in just off Camden Square. Getting the basement ready, and planning, shopping for and preparing lunch every day, were part of the curriculum (home economics), and so was attending meetings to discuss the running of the school (current events – citizenship, we'd call it now). The day started at 10.30, giving the virtually unparented, bedtime-less kids a chance to get up – after I had battled with the total-freedom fraction of the by-now sizeable Free School Committee for any start time at all. At least, I insisted, the kids would be able to practise getting up if any of them ever wanted to hold down a job. Autocrat, they murmured. How many of them were committing time to the free school, aside from coming to meetings, I asked. Fascist, they muttered, but almost all of them faded away. Their time was almost entirely devoted to political meetings of one sort or another. Roger had just discovered that the editorial board of *Children's Rights*, which consisted of a Reichian analyst and several of his patients, was more interested in the encouragement of active childhood sexuality than rights as such. He resigned, went on the dole (that, again) and became the school's first full-time teacher.

For some of the kids, it was a couple of years since

they had been in school. Allie, the thirteen-year-old, had gone back once, but during registration the class teacher was so used to her not being there that she hadn't bothered to call out her name, so Allie left before the first lesson and never went back. The two youngest children, aged seven and six, were just launching on their career of absenteeism, but the whole family, eleven in all, were in danger of being institutionalised. The police had a long-term plan for this criminal family, all of whom, even the youngest, regularly broke into the gentrified houses that had sprung up in the formerly working-class area and stole whatever electronic items appealed to them – while the little ones found chocolates, gorged themselves, and ground the surplus into the stripped and polished wooden floors. The two oldest brothers, aged sixteen and seventeen, were due in court the same week for attempted robbery of a post office, a plan that came to the attention of the law when they were caught with a sawn-off shotgun in a stolen van on their way to the job, because they were speeding. I thought at worst the free school might educate the younger kids to be more thoughtful criminals. We went to the local police station about getting the oldest boys bail. The sooner the whole family were locked up, the police told us, the better it would be for society (not so long afterwards, society would be declared non-existent, though this didn't seem to improve relations between the radically impoverished and the wealthy).

Both Mr and Mrs B. were alcoholics, usually out of

work, and completely baffled by life. There was an almost new fridge without a door rusting in the garden. Mrs B had got it from social services, but just afterwards she heard about a newspaper report of a child who had climbed into a fridge and suffocated, because the door had locked behind him and there was no way of opening it from the inside. Mrs B, in a moment of concerned parenthood, had taken the door off the fridge. When it turned out that the fridge no longer worked (because without a door it was no longer a fridge), she chucked it out into the garden. She didn't show up in court the day the two older boys' case came up. Roger and I went round early, but she was more or less unconscious from a night of drinking, and we couldn't rouse her. The eldest boy was sentenced to prison, and the younger one was given yet another period of probation, on the condition that we kept an eye on him and he helped out with the younger kids in the free school. In fact, none of them minded much about going to prison or borstal. They quite liked the regular hours and meals, and being kept busy during the day in the kitchen or laundry or workshops.

Roger besieged Camden Council, and I followed in his slipstream, marching through the corridors of the Town Hall and barging into offices, explaining that we were saving the local community an enormous amount of money by keeping the B. children and their friend out of care, and asking for a grant so that we could continue doing so. We weren't arrested, not even thrown out. These days, of course, we wouldn't have got past security at the front entrance. It was a lesson in persistence. After producing formal written proposals and making it clear that we weren't going to go away, we met with the then Councillor Frank Dobson (later to be a minister in the New Labour government), who headed up the Education Committee. He saw our financial argument, if nothing else, and put the case to the Council. Finally, we were given an astonishingly large grant of £20,000 for the year (far more than we'd asked for), on condition that we based the school on the nearby, presently disused sixteen-acre freightliner site behind King's Cross Station, and set up other useful social amenities along with the school – an old people's lunch club, an evening youth club, and a women's centre. While we were at it, we also started an urban farm – pigs, donkeys, goats, chickens – and sold manure to local gardeners. Suddenly we had an empire to run. Camden Local Education Authority sent its senior school inspector. The kids made him lunch, he sat in on the lessons, squeezed into Roger's fifteen-year-old Morris 1000 with some of the kids to go to an exhibition, and two weeks later passed the school as 'efficient', meaning that it was on a par as a teaching establishment with school for the time being. All done through energy. But achieved because it was still the tail-end of the Sixties and it wasn't impossible.

~

It started to occur to me by the late Sixties, once getting stoned stopped feeling like I was doing something, that there was nothing more important to be involved in and to get right than the education of children. It still strikes me as true, though my belief in the possibility of its achievement is close to zero now. I wasn't alone in the Sixties and early Seventies. Acknowledging the centrality of education to any improvement in society (that word again, its dying gasp) didn't require an excess of hard thinking, and the idea of children's rights caught on as other rights – gender, racial, social class – were demanded. If ever any group was unrepresented, powerless and without a concerted voice in society, it was children. The Children's Rights movement allowed anyone to project. Even if we had never been a woman, black or working-class, we had all been children, and recalled that outraged helplessness at the adult world being arbitrary and unfair towards us. We had been children not so very long ago. It was easy to recollect how stifling and trivial much of our education had been, and how it failed to engage anyone without strong motivation or exceptional schooling: either of which usually meant having the good fortune to have access to resources most people lacked – books, money, parents who had benefited themselves from learning, or parents who had missed out on it and were therefore passionate about it for their children. If we hadn't been sidelined by education, we knew most people had been. Those of us who had been to state schools had watched the sidelined ones slip away into no-hope streams; some of those who had been to private schools understood the extent of their privilege and suffered survivor guilt. We perceived the world as irrelevant and unjust to the majority, and the manifestation of irrelevance and injustice in the schools was closest to what most of us knew.

Those who were students – at university, college, art school – tried out radical education on themselves to start with. In America there was far more student unrest much earlier than in the UK, centring around resistance to the Vietnam war. The brutality with which demonstrations were dealt with by the police and authorities was astonishing to those of us who watched. Four students died from bullet wounds at Kent State, and suddenly being a student didn't seem to be simply a way of passing from childhood to adulthood with a period of blithe irresponsibility. The adults were killing their children, not just by sending them to war, but by shooting them for complaining about it. There was a general resentment of students around the world. It looked as if the grown-ups had got fed up with funding their young for a period of wildness. Perhaps there comes a point where the old simply resent the young and the fact the world will belong to them, rather than wanting to indulge them with what they had missed themselves. It does look at present as if the nostalgia my generation has for their Sixties is joined by our disapproval for the contemporary young – 'You only care about money, career and status. When we were young...' In the early Seventies, at any rate, it seemed that wildness was getting out of hand. Not just sex, drugs and rock and roll, but they were messing about in politics, too. The young were messing with the order of things, and on the old ones' money. So they sent in the cops. This gave students in America, and by association, around the world the chance to take themselves seriously.

They took over lecture halls and classrooms and refused to move. Sit-ins became teach-ins, and political speeches made room for an experimental pedagogy: students and some lecturers thought about sharing knowledge rather than having it poured into them to be regurgitated again during exams. The politics of education as well as the need for a political education caught fire and lit up the imagination as a way to shake the world into a better shape. The idea of voluntary learning grew into the thought that curricula should be as much the responsibility of the student as the teacher. The magisterial application of knowledge to the young was no longer self-evident. What this meant, of course, was an exponential growth of meetings and talk. The official educators and administrators were locked out, and the buildings were commandeered for lengthy debates in classrooms, lecture theatres and cafeterias among striking students about what should be learned, how it should be learned and who should teach it. At its best, it was a useful period of reassessment, but it was also a party, an avoidance, and a gift to the more dogmatic and pedantic students who differed from the authoritarian establishment only in their age and access to official power. There was much talk of cutting through the bullshit which was being taught in schools and colleges that had stopped pupils and students from thinking about what they were doing and why, and there was certainly also a good deal of bullshit talked. The accusations from establishment educators and politicians of self-indulgence were true, but that will and energy to look at the nature of what should be learned and how also represented the best of what the Sixties were about. The press berated the students for abusing the privilege of education and the grants they received from the society which they so disparaged, but this was exactly what the students should have been doing. When the young keep their heads down for fear of failing exams and not getting highly-paid jobs, they are not taking their privilege of learning seriously. For all that these were privileged people (all students are regarded as privileged, even by those who were once students themselves) in a time of full employment, in the Sixties the young at least risked those privileges to investigate what it was they were doing, rather than simply accept what they were told. Most dissenting students got back on the bourgeois straight and narrow, we are told, just as the majority of the radicals became card-carrying members of conventional society. But that doesn't prove, as it is sometimes held to, that they were wrong-headed in their briefly wayward youth. The young have a job to do of frightening the grown-ups.

And what could frighten the grown-ups more than subverting the education system of those who have yet to become students? The change-over from the two-tier grammar/secondary moderns to comprehensive schools* that began under Harold Wilson in 1965 had speeded up, and by 1970, in spite of the new Conservative government and Margaret Thatcher becoming Secretary of State for Education, the dismantling of the old system was unstoppable. The division of children at the age of eleven by examination into either academic or 'practical' schools (to become university students or to leave school at fifteen respectively[†]) had largely gone, but mixed-ability teaching was an untried and under-researched discipline and the result usually was that both ends of the ability spectrum were short-changed. By the end of the decade, the comprehensive system was far from proving itself a force for social equality and liberal education. Many schools had given up and divided year groups into separate classes according to academic ability. Grammar and secondary modern schools coexisted in effect within the comprehensives. Nobody really knew what they were doing and it was showing. At the East End comprehensive where I taught, each year was split into seven groups labelled with one letter of the word HACKNEY. In order to prevent the children from being demoralised

---

*Previously all children in the State system took an exam at eleven, the results of which filtered those who passed to academic grammar schools, and those who failed to 'practical' secondary modern schools, where a good deal of woodwork and metalwork was on the curriculum. Comprehensive schools were mixed-ability schools that children attended on the basis of locality, not an exam. The eleven-plus was abolished with a few exceptions.

† The school leaving age was raised to sixteen in 1973.

by finding themselves in the bottom two groups (which were designated by the teachers 'remedial'), each year started at the other end of the word. 1H, 1A, 1C, 1K, 1N, 1E, 1Y became 2Y, 2E, 2N, 2K, 2C, 2A, 2H the following year. Not even the poorest of intellects could fail to know where they were in the ability hierarchy. In Islington, a passionately child-centred, progressive headteacher Michael Duane, had tried to put ideals into practice at Risinghill Comprehensive. In 1965 it was closed down as an experiment out of control. The book that came out about it in 1968 made Duane a hero, and Risinghill a rallying cry, though there were serious problems with Duane's new lack of order, as there had been with the old excess of it.[17]

The comprehensive system had stopped looking like an experiment in the liberation of working-class children and seemed already to be achieving little more than providing a minimally educated workforce for an industrial economy. The power of institutions to make even new ideas conform to the requirements of the status quo was evident, but we were still close enough to the Sixties and our youth to believe that it could be subverted. Schools and schooling became a cause among the young liberal and radical Left. Teachers, students and academics considered alternative forms of teaching. The question was again what should be taught and how pupils could participate in their own learning. Education under the dead hand of the institution deprived children of the social and philosophical freedom to think, often even of the ability to obtain basic literacy and numeracy – a serious problem that comprehensive schools have still not solved. The majority of children were leaving school with just enough knowledge to take up the unskilled jobs society needed doing. Those who call themselves realists and pragmatists will tell you, then and now, that that is precisely the purpose of state education. We chose to believe (and I still like us for it) that everyone was capable of doing better than that – of having broader horizons, and of being educated into a wide curiosity that might mean they were dissatisfied with their lot, but which also gave them the tools for independent thought.

This, of course, was the paternalism of an educated youthful elite with world-changing on their mind, who rejoiced in dissent, having enjoyed several years of living it without the fear of long-term unemployment. Or, to put it another way, it was an imaginative merging of us and the children (only a few years apart in age). The Peter Pan generation were trying to give our younger selves the liberated childhood we had belatedly discovered and were presently acting out, just as our parents had funded us to have a carefree misspent youth that they had lacked. Idealistically, numbers of us enlisted in the education system (in those days, just having a degree qualified you to become a teacher, and for those of us who didn't have degrees, there were teacher training colleges and, of course, grants to attend them that could be lived on). Not having been to university, I got a grant and started teacher training, while postgraduates went directly to work in inner-city comprehensive schools which by now had major problems with discipline and motivation. Sink schools, they were being called by the panicking press. We would work in the system, at the tough end, work with the kids, on their side, and change things radically. We weren't disciplinarian or jealous of our status, so we talked to the pupils and required dialogue in return. On the whole, it worked rather well; we had to do less ducking to avoid chairs being thrown than our colleagues who enforced pointless rules and shouted their theoretical authority at kids who didn't believe a word of it and couldn't care less. We may have done more social work than actual teaching, but our classroom discipline techniques, which mostly involved taking a non-combative stance and actually liking the kids, were quite effective, and we thought that once we'd got them quiet enough to listen we could say some things that mattered. Our logic was as compelling as that which had made us already believe we would change everything just by our novel presence in the reactionary world. It was a takeover, but an inevitable one. A generational takeover, by the generation that thought differently. The kids would recognise our benevolent and socially radical intentions and join us in the endeavour. Institutions couldn't resist our will if we participated in them. Now we got the idea of 'boring from within'. They would become *our* institutions, new, compassionate, world-changing, and above all equitable. We'd done drugs, expanded our minds, read and trekked the world, east and west, and now we were going to teach. Obvious really. Of course, we had many moments of discouragement – it turned out there were some kids who didn't want our benevolence at all, and sometimes we had to duck chairs along with the oldest and most unregenerated of our colleagues. A fellow world-changer, a member of IS, who taught remedial classes (EY or HA according to the year), slammed into the staffroom one breaktime and threw herself despairingly into a chair, announcing, 'These kids are no good for socialism' – but, for all that, how could we not prevail in the end?

Ivan Illich, a former turbulent priest who had worked in Latin America, thought otherwise. In 1971, he published *Deschooling Society*.[18] His target in this and his other books was the institution, by which he meant institutions of every kind – educational, technological, industrial, medical: the divisive and divided fortresses of knowledge itself. The institutions aped and were always and unalterably governed by economic forces for their own benefit. There was no possibility of changing the world by tinkering with the institutions that controlled it. The nature of education had to change fundamentally, he said. I read Illich, as well as others[19] who advocated the idea of taking education into the hands of the local community, of creating new, small institutions, rethinking the content and meaning of learning, and I somehow managed to participate both in the noble idea of changing education from within its fortifications, and the new free school/community school movement. While I did the required teacher training, I was intensely involved in the (somewhat unintentional) Freightliners Free School. It wasn't contradictory, to my mind. The free school would be the ideal practice (a live experiment, not a rehearsal as were the teaching practices of the training colleges) for the changes that we would implement in the comprehensives to turn them into the humane, creative institutions they ought to be. But I was not reading Illich very carefully. I (and others) misread his clear statements of libertarianism as liberalism.

> Universal education through schooling is not feasible. It would be no more feasible if it were attempted by means of alternative institutions built on the style of present schools. Neither new attitudes of teachers toward their pupils nor the proliferation of educational hardware or software (in classroom or bedroom), nor finally the attempt to expand the pedagogue's responsibility until it engulfs his pupils' lifetimes will deliver universal education.[20]

Neither the Free School movement, nor the new influx of radical teachers into the comprehensive system, had suggested *not* teaching. We were trying for *good* teaching, better and wider teaching. It wasn't what Illich was on about at all.

> The free-school movement entices unconventional educators, but ultimately does so in support of the conventional ideology of schooling…Even the seemingly radical critics of the school system are not willing to abandon the idea that they have an obligation to the

young, especially to the poor, an obligation to process them, whether by love or by fear...And there is, finally, a shared view of youth which is psychologically romantic and politically conservative. According to this view, changes in society must be brought about by burdening the young with the responsibility of transforming it – but only after their eventual release from school.[21]

Rereading Illich now, I wonder what happened in my head, back in 1971, when I got to those passages? Did I simply not see them? Did I refuse to read them in such a way that what they actually said entered my consciousness? His analysis of the result of liberals taking over the schools was precise and accurate, it was to turn out, but it was paralysing unless the economic and industrial reality we lived in was torn into small pieces. People would only be free when they educated themselves and each other *all at the same level*. Illich was too radical for the radical generation. We were not so idealistic that we trusted in Illich's radical alteration of society ever happening. And though we didn't want to see ourselves as part of the old reactionary system, nor, truth be told, did we want to risk losing control of what we valued. We supposed, without quite articulating it, that left to itself, a self-educated population would fail to notice the literature, philosophy and art of which we thought so highly. Illich didn't care whether they noticed or not. He wasn't coming from a left/liberal position. He wasn't interested in making things nice, or expanding minds according to anyone's view of how minds should or could be expanded.

I took my fifteen-year-old class from Hackney on a school trip to the Roundhouse to see the radical and often-naked Living Theatre company from the US perform. I thought that my pupils' dropping jaws at the sights and sounds they encountered would function in a similar way to the Methedrine the psychiatrists at the Maudsley injected into my veins. That they would be abreacted into art. But the absolute freedom of the individual was Ivan Illich's only interest, whatever its consequences.

> The right of free assembly has been politically recognised and culturally accepted. We should now understand that this right is curtailed by laws that make some form of assembly obligatory. This is especially the case with institutions which conscript according to age group, class, or sex, and which are very time consuming. The army is one example. School is an even more outrageous one.[22]

We wanted small, local groupings of teachers and learners, not none at all. His 'web' of learning was a loose, always shifting network, that depended not on any kind of qualification or well-meaning, but only on individuals who simultaneously and freely wanted knowledge and offered knowledge, and who needed only to be provided with the means (an imagined universal computerised access) for each to get in touch with the other. That was the point, to dispense completely with structure, to undercut the authority of hierarchy and the hierarchy of authority. Crucially, the majority of the activists in my generation were never as interested in individual liberty as we were in finding ways to implement our own ideas of how the world should be. I'm not sure, on Illich's still startlingly strict definition, if we were interested in liberty at all. Certainly, we didn't *get* that 'freedom' was not solely the property of the liberal Left. Yet again, aside from a rigorous few, we were too young, and not thinking coldly enough, to imagine what a Margaret Thatcher might do with the word. Illich could well have joined Thatcher and Reagan's theoretical advisers. I'd resist the claim that the Sixties generation were responsible for the Thatcher years, as I would resist the notion that the Jewish community in Germany were responsible for the advent of the Nazis, but sometimes I can't help but see how unwittingly we might have been sweeping the path in readiness for the radical Right, preparing, with the best of good intentions, the road to hell for paving.

I think perhaps we were also romanticising some nebulously defined educational processes at the cost of a simpler acquisition of basic skills. The intention was to get children engaged in learning, interested in what they were doing without having to be competitive. Learning how to learn, rather than learning the same old facts without being given an understanding of the basis of them. Ideas which in my view are still admirable, and still sorely lacking in education systems, but in noticing the barriers to education we rejected some kinds of learning that simply made life easier. We hadn't, most of us, by then, had children of our own to observe. The fact is that young children are wonderfully programmed for learning by rote. Why understand the alphabet or times tables, when you can chant them meaninglessly and learn them fast to have at will for the rest of your life? Child-centred education was, at least in part, our own misty eyes centring on our wishful thinking about childhood. We had all learned to read by reciting the alphabet, and sing-songed the multiplication tables until we had them off by heart, and can still call them up whenever needed, even in our sixties chanting the alphabet or the eight times table in our heads in moments of need. We made life more difficult, I think, in respect of elementary learning, for both pupil and teacher by demanding that everything had to be understood. Get the automatic stuff under your belt and then you can have all the time in the world to sit back and learn to understand it to your heart's content, is what I would say now. And I do wonder if the awful educational backlash of the subsequent Thatcher and post-Thatcher Blair years that continues to demand efficiency over content, measurable outcomes becoming everything, were not, in part, fuelled by our over-emphasis on making the relevance of every aspect of learning a priority. We forgot what pleasure we had had from irrelevance, from the strange and the half-understood, and even from the difficult. There was also an embarrassment about our own abilities, the gifts of our own minds. We tended devotedly to the lower end of the ability spectrum but paid little attention to the more able. They were us, after all, and we were quite ashamed of our privileges. It got to the point where in some sense we punished the brighter kids for not being underprivileged. When Allie had been at the free school for a while, she became very taken with looking at buildings in a new way that had been pointed out to her on school visits round London with the local architect. She began to think she might want to be an architect. She told this to one of the play-leaders at the adventure playground whom she had known and been friends with in the days when she bunked off school all the time. 'You're getting a bit above yourself, aren't you?' he said. The radicals couldn't always cope with education actually having an effect. If the oppressed stopped behaving like the oppressed, we didn't really like it. And there was another side. One day Allie came to me and said she wanted to go back to regular school. I said that was fine if it was what she wanted, but I wondered why. 'I want to be like my mates,' she said. 'I want to bunk off like they do. With Freightliners being our special school I have to keep on going to it, and I just want to be normal.'

We were a generation that wanted to give the children the childhoods we wished we had had, or thought we wished we had had. Unless the easy access we had to the dole and those generous education grants was, after all, a covert gift driven by a similar wish in the older generation, we were different from our parents. And we have turned out to be different from our children. Both those generations, older and younger than us, were and are more inclined than we were to reproduce for their young what they experienced in their childhood, rather than offer them Wonderland. We were stardust, we were golden and we had to get ourselves back to the garden ...

6

CHANGING OUR MINDS

If I don't know I don't know, I think I know. If I don't
know I know I know, I think I don't know.

R. D. Laing, *Knots*, 1970

Clon wore – it was still somewhat notable in 1969 – a ring
in one ear, and his hair was dirty blond, falling in careless curls around his face and neck like Shelley's, though
his overall look was more piratical than poetic. When
asked what it was short for, he repeated that his name
was Clon. 'Just Clon,' he insisted, in a way that suggested
it wasn't. He was bold and handsome in a roguish way,
and his startling clear blue eyes looked directly at you,
always amused, and with, it seemed, a rock-solid con-
fidence in himself that didn't require yours because he
had enough of his own. Compared to the rest of us, he
seemed to glow internally.

I was one of about thirty patients at the Paddington
Day Clinic, an experiment in intensive group therapy, set
up and funded by the local Health Authority, at Royal
Oak in West London. A committee of elected patients
interviewed prospective patients after one of the two
psychiatrists in charge had done so and passed on to
us those they thought could benefit from joining the
emotional scrummage. New people were only admitted if they passed their second interview. Admission

committees generally admit those most like themselves, so it was a fairly homogeneous group: young, very few people over twenty-five, disturbed, angry, dysfunctional, but often talented in a wasted, wayward sort of way, and highly articulate. Not much point in a full-time regime of group therapy from nine to five, five days a week, if people weren't able to express themselves. We undertook not to take any drugs, including prescription tranquillisers and anti-depressants, and to participate in the various large and small groups that went on during the day. It was a place of high and constant drama. Everyone, some time or other, had their moment as the centre (or victim) of the group's attention – anyone who didn't volunteer to talk about themselves and their problem and have it considered by everyone else would, after a period of grace, be challenged and confronted on their silence. It could be very harsh. There were tears, arguments, walkouts, collapses and sometimes violence. Relations within the community, general and sexual, were examined with scalpels. The skin of everything was lifted back to look at the bloody mess that inevitably lay beneath. Every day brought smaller or larger crises and emotional turmoil. You really needed to be quite tough or hooked on emotional turmoil to survive it. Some of us were very troubled, others less obviously so, but if you got through the rather gruelling, unsympathetic patients' committee interview, it was reckoned you could cope. Mostly, this was right, but during my four months there one or two people attempted suicide rather than talk (or as a result of it); others spoke out and, finding themselves over-whelmed by the effort or the response, left, sometimes for less experimental psychiatric inpatient care. There were those who watched, for as long as they could get away with it, and those who made themselves the centre of the group as much as they could get away with it. It was an education in group dynamics if you were a watcher, but there was always someone watching you and sooner rather than later you would be dragged into the collective eye of the group. If you denied the accusation of evasion or defended yourself, you were not facing up to your problems, or you were aggressive and not facing up to your problems; if you agreed with others' assessments, you were too compliant and probably concealing the real issue. Breaking down, one way or another, was pretty much a requirement; a proof that you were 'working'.

Clon lasted longer than any of the watchers – even me. He was never successfully enticed or goaded into the centre of a group session. He sat with his bold, knowing smile on his face and spoke neither on someone else's problems or his own. If asked directly for a comment or how he felt, he'd shrug and open his blue eyes wide. 'I'm cool, man.' He had an exceptional capacity to resist being drawn in. Partly it was his compelling charm, and a mysterious ability to deflect attention as if he had a mir-rored surface that enquiry slid off harmlessly and on to whomever else his eyes might turn towards. But it was also because of the confusion he created by the fiend-ishly cunning puzzle he set the community. I was on the

committee that admitted him. His answer to the standard question 'Why do you think you would benefit from
joining this community?' was instant and direct, spoken
with a broad open-faced grin: 'Because I'll get a medical
certificate and the sickness benefit, man.'

It was a novel response. All patients did get a medical
certificate for as long as they were with the clinic to say
that they were unfit for work by virtue of a psychological
disorder and were entitled to about (I think) £7 a week
state benefit. But everyone, including Clon, had been
referred to the clinic by an outside psychiatrist as needing
treatment and being potentially suitable for this particular experimental form. And nearly everyone given the
opportunity at the admission interview to itemise their
neuroses and psychoses had to be silenced eventually,
or there would be nothing left to tell the group if we let
them in. So we laughed at Clon's casual joke. Yeah, funny,
but, really, what was his problem?

'I haven't got one. Really. I heard about this place and
it's, like, perfect. I want to hang out here and get paid
same as you guys. I'm cool, man. Happy childhood, life's
great. But it would be better if I didn't have to get a job.'
He smiled amiably as he spoke, as if we were all in on the
scam and knew exactly what he was talking about.

'No,' said the chair of our committee. 'Seriously.'

'Seriously,' said Clon. 'They've chucked me off the
dole and I don't want to work. I want to be like you cats.'

He had nothing to add. He gave a bland account of
being brought up I can't remember where, nothing

interesting, no problems, just didn't want a job and had heard about the clinic. He went to his doctor, saw a shrink, said what he had to say to be referred, and here he was. Smiling. Coming clean, wanting some of what we'd got.

'Why should we admit you if you've really got nothing wrong with you?'

'Why not? What's it to you if I hang around here for a while?'

Bristling, the committee chairman said that everyone here was entitled to be here because they had serious and genuine problems and needed psychiatric help. He would be taking the place of someone who needed treatment. Clon kept his face locked into a smile, while he threw in his ace.

'Yeah, well, how do you know I'm not faking it… the not being crazy?'

We sent him out of the room so we could discuss his application. It should have taken seconds to come to a decision, and for one or two people there was nothing to talk about. But there was another view. Clon's brilliant skill at concealing his problems made him an ideal candidate for the clinic. Obviously, he had severe problems – he had been sent here by a doctor, passed on to us by our psychiatrists – and anyone who insisted that they had no mental problems, in general and in particular to the admission committee, was either really deluded or crying out for help to uncover their inner horror. He had virtually told us, with a sneer that by no means meant it wasn't true, not to take him at his own word. Wouldn't we be failing him if we rejected him? Colluding with his refusal to face the painful truth about himself? He was in.

For weeks great efforts went on within the large morning and evening group and the smaller groups that continued through the day to get Clon to confront his problems.

'Clon, everyone has their difficulties. You've seen how people open up here. There's no shame in admitting your fears. We're here to help. You have to work on your stuff, like everyone else.'

'Yeah, well, I would, but I don't have any problems. I'm having a great time. If you're bothered by me, that's your problem. I'm getting what I want. This is fun and I'm being paid.'

It was true there was no evidence that Clon was other than quite content sitting in the groups, drinking tea, having lunch, hanging out until five o'clock. He wasn't moody or given to sudden violence, weeping in corners, turning over tables, or screaming at someone he could no longer tolerate. He tolerated us perfectly, even seemed to enjoy himself, without ever actually participating with issues of his own or commenting on those of anyone else. Eventually, the admissions committee met to decide whether to expel Clon. He was summoned. All he had to do was say that he was fucked up like the rest of us.

'Hey, I told you the truth and you admitted me. How can you expel me now? Nothing's changed.'

He was right. The question was whether Clon was

madder than all of us or a brilliant con artist. Yet he wasn't exactly conning us. He certainly wasn't pretending to be mad. But was he pretending *not* to be mad? Or – was he pretending to *be* mad by claiming not to be mad? He was a maestro of the double bind. Ronnie Laing would have loved him. But there were other ways, easier ways of getting social security, without having to sit through day after day of people having tantrums and obsessing about their inner demons. And even if he was just using the place, might it not teach him something in spite of himself? The big question kept returning: was he or wasn't he authentic? I found myself wondering why it mattered so much to us. Having accepted him, shouldn't we let him stay? And what the hell if he *was* playing the system? I had a kind of respect for his position, whatever it was, or really was. But then I'm the daughter of a conman. It was a long meeting. Finally, he was expelled. The danger that we were being taken for a ride (even though, or because, we couldn't be sure what kind of ride we were being taken for) was too great for us to risk. As Clon had said over and over again in group: it was our problem. We called Clon in and told him he was out. I remember his shrug, and the who-cares, it-lasted-as-long-as-it-lasted beaming smile on his face.

'Well, fuck you, then,' he said, not entirely amicably, and swaggered out of the room, out of the building, never to be seen again.

I'm still not sure whether I imagine in sentimental retrospect or actually saw a brief look of fear cross his face before he cleared it, or if his shrug wasn't exactly the kind of shrug I used to make as an adolescent when I was given up on yet again, and all that mattered was to show that I didn't care one bit.

~

I'd been sent to the day clinic after a consultation with Aaron Esterson, who had co-authored *Sanity, Madness and the Family,* Volume 1 of the proposed series *Families of Schizophrenics,* with R. D. Laing in 1964. In 1965, *The Divided Self,* written by Laing alone and originally published in 1960, was published in the Pelican series of books – that lifeline of paperback knowledge and information of every discipline which adorned the period and, along with the system of free public libraries, gave those of us who had rejected or been rejected by a university education, a way to learn. It was the beginning of the anti-psychiatry movement of the Sixties. *Families of Schizophrenics* proposed the theory that it was families who were mad rather than simply the individuals who were scapegoated by them as the 'sick member'. The case histories taken by Laing and Esterson were chilling and strangely familiar whether you came from a recognisably mad family or one you had been brought up to think of as 'normal'. *The Divided Self* extended this to suggesting that society itself estranged the mad, and caused them to create false selves in order to survive. From this position, it was a short hop, given the ethos of the Sixties, to doubting the normality of normality itself and then to questioning the madness of madness. The qualities of sanity or madness were defined as 'degrees of conjunction and disjunction between two persons where the one is sane by common consent'.[23] Laing was brilliant and was taken up by the intelligentsia, as well as, when they differed, the desperate. Admirers gathered at his feet at parties to listen to him talk about his theories. He drank heavily and took to using LSD frequently. His book *The Politics of Experience and The Bird of Paradise*[24] confirmed the holy-madness/consecrated-drugs connection. Enlightenment found another branch: drugs were already a fast route to opening ourselves up to the religious experience of Eastern philosophy, now they became a way for those not 'blessed' with madness to get an insight into this newly hallowed state. From being victims of their families, the mad* became the victims of society in general, and its medical institutions in particular (in timely line with the concurrently translated writings of Foucault). The mad – the word became a banner of resistance – were outcasts, prophets, speakers of unspeakable truths, and were pronounced heroes. Pushed by malign normality, the mad, on behalf of those of us who hadn't the courage, took a journey to the furthest depths of the human psyche to look at what was really there, and who we really were. They

---

*Schizophrenics, specifically; those of us who were depressives were merely dull.

---

trod the lonely hero's journey (a classic quest scenario, also in vogue through the new popularity of Joseph Campbell's *Hero with a Thousand Faces*[25]) beyond the boundaries of society to places most of us dared not go, and they returned changed but with news of the truth they had found and brought back for us if we would just pay proper attention. When schizophrenics babbled or screamed or wept about their voices and told terrified tales of being spied on by MI6 or SMERSH, of being the risen Christ recrucified, or Satan cast down again, they were, Laing said, to be listened to on their own terms, creatively understood, translated like radio messages from the Resistance, not medicated and institutionalised back to numbness – the numbness of the so-called-sane, now revealed to be a contemptible state of willed ignorance. The mad were the super-sane. We couldn't hear them because we were not sensitive enough, or we couldn't bear to face the truth they spoke about our own 'normality'. Just as we were later to discover ourselves to be racist and sexist, so, in the mid-Sixties, we were to understand ourselves as madist. Not only should we stop persecuting the mad, we needed to *become* mad in order to achieve real sanity.

It was incredibly seductive. The mad hero became a teacher, whose pronouncements were only for those who could or would understand. The crazy were shamans, gurus, speakers in tongues, cut loose from ordinary language and behaviour, and were at risk, as are all holy men and women, of persecution from being locked up and drugged into silence. They were the heirs to the witch hunts conducted by the Inquisition. Society found the mad intolerable and psychically killed them if they refused to conform. They spoke the peculiar language of truth, a kind of poetry, and acted out reality, inscrutable to those who refused to hear and see. Laing and fellow psychotherapists David Cooper and Joseph Burke opened a house in East London, called Kingsley Hall, where the shrinks and the mad lived communally and defied uninitiated visitors to tell which was which. It wasn't that easy to tell even for those who lived there. Mary Barnes was a famous resident: a former nurse who had had a catastrophic breakdown in her mid-forties. In the basement of Kingsley Hall, she painted frantic pictures in swirling psychedelic colours, howled, ranted, was reborn, nursed dolls at her breast, shat like a baby and rubbed it into the walls. Everything was permitted. Everything expressed the message about reality she was trying to get across. It was a private healing process from which the 'normal' could benefit just by watching and reading about it.[26] The Good Doctors were there not to control but to enable whatever needed to happen so that the mad could express themselves. If a 'patient' took off her clothes during a session, Laing took off his too in order to show that he was on her wavelength. Wavelength was everything, though I'm inclined to doubt now that the mad really wanted their doctors to be as mad as they were. Laing and the other anti-psychiatrists provided hash, mescaline and LSD to open the channels to the truth, in much the same spirit that a handful of other people, responding to similar spiritual and psychological teaching at the time, were trepanning themselves – boring holes in their foreheads in order to let the light into their third eye.

And let me say, for all its excesses and cock-ups and carelessnesses, even the stupidities, the anti-psychiatry movement had a point. Life for the institutionalised mad was grim. In the huge hospitals for the mad, left over from the Victorians, they were drugged into silence and calamitous palsies, received electroshock therapy and lobotomies, well into the Sixties and beyond. In spite of the worthy Quakers of the nineteenth century, care for the mad in large asylums was often brutal and punitive, suffering from a lack of good training and money. What mental institutions did for many people was institutionalise them. Going into the madhouse often trained the mad to want to remain incarcerated. It is not accidental that in Ken Kesey's book *One Flew Over the Cuckoo's Nest*,[27] the great revelatory moment is when the Clon-like hero, McMurphy, discovers that all his fellow victims are voluntary patients, and not, like him, on a section. They could all leave if they wanted to.

I was certainly ready for anti-psychiatry. I had been in two psychiatric hospitals when I read *The Divided Self*, and was shortly to be in a third. I never suffered from brutality, but I saw its effects on staff and other patients. Geriatric patients and those we would now call sufferers of Alzheimer's disease were lumped in with psychiatric patients: they were particularly hard to cope with and got roughly handled. When I objected at one woman, in her late forties with an early form of dementia, who incessantly roamed round and round the day room, whimpering, being pushed into her chair, I was told to mind my own business: 'You're just a patient.' Mostly, I was on anti-depressants and saw a psychiatrist twice a week for fifteen minutes (having seen the terrors of those who had ECT when I was fifteen, I always refused to have it), but in one hospital I was put into 'sleep therapy' after it was decided I was particularly depressed, and when a nurse noticed several days later that I was suffering from barbiturate poisoning as a result, and I became 'difficult' to deal with, wanting more of the lovely oblivion I had been given, I was detained under a section of the Mental Health Act that deprived me of any right to agree or disagree with my own treatment and the right to leave. I was detained, literally, being held down by several nurses and injected with Largactyl, which put me into another narcosis, but this time with hideous nightmares I couldn't wake up from. Later, in the Maudsley, it was the 'abreaction' therapy and intravenous injections of methylamphetamine. A woman in the bed next to me, incredibly in 1968, was put on the completely discredited insulin shock therapy, another given LSD 'treatment'. Two or three of the patients had received lobotomies, and sat passively waiting to be discharged. The strangest things were going on. And all the time, in all the hospitals, I watched people come back from their twentieth, thirtieth, God knows how many, electro-convulsive therapy session, pale, horrified and remembering nothing about themselves or where they were, but weeping with fear as the next ECT became due. Psychiatrists I've talked to since, some of them working later at the Maudsley, are amazed to hear about the treatment I saw and received, but the hospital was a teaching hospital and regarded itself as being on the experimental edge.

Laing's ideas came when the time was absolutely right for them. Politics was experience, experience was political. I saw people not being healed, but kept quiet, being made more convenient, sometimes with the best will in the world, but always, it seemed to me, with ears and eyes closed to what the distressed and the mad were actually experiencing. I read Laing's books as if they were a road map of my life. I wanted to be part of it (even though I was just a humble depressive and he was only really interested in exciting schizophrenics). But when, as an outpatient at the Tavistock Clinic in the mid-Sixties, I said that I wanted to go and work as a volunteer at Kingsley Hall, my psychiatrist responded (quite correctly, of course, it wouldn't have been very good for my own mental health), 'If you try, I'll have you sectioned.' The threat to lock up and give enforced treatment to wilful patients was always readily available in the psychiatrist's medical bag and a gift to any anti-authoritarian patient or theoretician.

Laing fused the notion of liberation of the insane with the buzz that was already beginning to be heard about the liberation of the mind in a broader sense, and it was thrillingly cogent. At least in theory. Laing was a brilliant theoretician; but as a practitioner, Dr Ronnie's patients were often dumped back into institutions or left to cope for themselves when they became too hard even for him to handle. He called in the men in white coats and walked away more than once to my knowledge. Drugs, drink, general craziness and a phenomenal amount of ego mixed with the theory and made some dangerous black holes in the practice.

Even aside from Laing's own limitations, there was the matter of pain. While we romanticised madness, he and those of us who supported him failed to take seriously the excruciating pain of the mad. Pain was existential truth, so the anti-psychiatrists permitted them to go through it; indeed, insisted that they did. In fact, as anyone stuck in the middle of a severe depression or a terrifying psychotic episode would have told their champions if they'd really been listening, people suffering from severe mental illness would do anything to make the anguish stop. Most of those having ECT, lobotomies, and mind-numbing drugs were voluntary patients, as McMurphy found out, prepared to have whatever treatment it would take to stop the nightmare. The anti-psychiatrists took other people's pain too philosophically. Nevertheless, for all that, read those early books by Laing and Esterson, even parts of Laing's later increasingly gnomic, not to say crazy, or faux-crazy writings, and see if they aren't still powerful, intelligent and compelling.

In just the same way as it happened with politics and education, liberation got confused with libertarianism. And in the area of psychiatry, too, Thatcher and Reagan in the Eighties took up our slack thinking, to transform the rhetoric and turn it into their own special form of radicalism, all the while blaming the chaos caused by the permissiveness of the Sixties for their harsh 'necessities'. We were guilty of woolly-mindedness: and as in politics and education, the upshot of libertarianism was there to be seen at the time. We didn't see it, or if we did, we didn't think about it enough. Thomas Szasz's book *The Myth of Mental Illness*,[28] was read as another book, along with those of Laing and friends, that promoted anti-psychiatry and the freeing of the mad from the shackles of the medicating doctors. It was, in its way. At least in theory. Mental illness was a category of control by institutions of the individual. Shut down the mental hospitals, free the madmen, they were no more mad than you and me, said Szasz. It looked on a not-careful-enough reading just like the liberating theses of the Good Doctors. How carefully did we read the passages where he said that if the so-called mad behaviour of those pushed out on to the streets was causing civil difficulties, it was simple misbehaviour, and should be treated as such: delinquents should be locked up in prisons, dealt with by courts? And perhaps it wasn't actually so far from Laing's position, certainly not so far from his practice. But it's easy to see now that this view (and perhaps, indeed, the Good Doctors' views) could sit happily to the far right of the political spectrum. Szasz wanted to get rid of the 'namby-pamby caring' that was precisely what us namby-pamby carers in the Sixties were wanting to achieve more of. We were (those of us not aligned to strict Marxist or Trotskyist groups who took more care in analysing what they were reading) profoundly naïve, the wishy-washy liberals, the wets, so sneered at by the Thatcher government. Thomas Szasz wanted no kind of doctoring at all of the mind. Let people be free to roam the streets and cause trouble, and let those who didn't like it deal with them as individual nuisances. There was no such distinction as bad or mad. The State had no business interfering with matters of the mind, or even supposing that Mind existed. Along with the behaviourist psychologists, like B. F. Skinner and John B. Watson, Szasz's point was to reject the notion that mind had any meaning at all. He didn't want to help the mad or listen to them, or offer them asylum; he wanted to abolish the idea of them. He refuted the concept of madness in order to refute any claim for civic responsibility towards others. Close the hospitals, let the mad walk free. Everyone made their own individual choices: the rich, the poor, the mad, the sane. That was their problem. Charles Shaar Murray assessed it correctly when in 1988, after the libertarian Right had done its worst, he noted:

> The line from hippy to yuppie is not nearly as convoluted as people like to believe and a lot of the old hippie rhetoric could well be co-opted now by the pseudo-libertarian Right – which has in fact happened. Get the government

off our backs, let individuals do what they want – that translates very smoothly into laissez-faire yuppyism, and that's the legacy of the era.[29]

The argument limps on, between generations now, about the legacy of the permissive Sixties. There are two accusations: that we caused the greed and self-interest of the Eighties by invoking the self, the individual, as the unit of society and setting up individualism for the Right to pick up and run with; or that we caused it by being so permissive, so soppy about matters that needed hard, firm handling, that a reaction was inevitable if the West wasn't to sink into a morass of self-indulgent chaos. But, we cry, that wasn't what we meant. And it wasn't. We had hardly invented the idea of Self, nor the idea that the individual had a right to respect and equality. Nor is it, anathema though it might be to the communitarian Left, such a terrible notion so long as the bad guys don't get hold of it. We were, and some of us still are, namby-pamby. We certainly believed very definitely that there was such a thing as society, and that attending to its most vulnerable members was one of its main tasks. But we were guilty, I think, of not imagining the Eighties, of not being able to visualise what David Widgery calls Thatcher's 'appalling candour'[30] in denouncing society as a myth, and the greed and self-interest (not the same thing as an interest in the self) that could be and was unleashed in the name of sacred individualism. We didn't really believe in the existence of the bad guys. We were guilty, too, of failing to understand the power of capitalism, the pull of material well-being, because many of us had had it much of our lives and could therefore easily enough imagine something different. We thought we would be happy to share our goods and our relationships. Mostly, we weren't, but even if we had been, the promise of wealth for all, of owning property rather than having housing provided by councils at fair rents, was too desirable for those that had been left out of ownership. And most people didn't have either the time or the inclination to devote themselves to listening for the underlying sense the mad might be making. They didn't want lives that included allowing individuals all the time in the world they needed to regress, to paint and to smear the walls with shit. They weren't interested in the mental travellers coming back with remarkable tales to tell; they wanted, as people seem always to want, to get on, and getting on meant focusing narrowly on the vital business of getting things (money, success, objects) and not worrying too much about those who didn't, unless they needed sequestering. Truth (whatever it may be), art (whatever that may be), consideration at a cost to yourself, none of those were priorities compared to a decent standard of living and the promise of ever better, ever more to come.

Whether it was our fault, or the fault of those other radicals of the Eighties and Nineties, the current situation seems to be that those who are looking to be in charge of the world next are actually facing the prospect of not much world at all. There are small signs that a new radicalism is developing, or at least desperate attempts, here and there, to resist the dying of the planet. Gathering force, I hope. The Sixties generation are getting to an age where the world is beginning to look quite baffling and alien. It happens to everyone as they grow older. People don't notice you in the street, they aren't very interested in what you have to say. We complain about how things used to be and how they are now – better then, terrible now. And it feels as if this is true. But perhaps it always feels true as the centre drifts away from you. Anyway, no one takes much notice – they make TV programmes called *Grumpy Old Men*, as we used to sit around laughing at Alf Garnett and his ever-baffled missus.*

What alarms me is how little has actually changed. There are new laws governing what can be said and ensuring that minorities are treated better in the workplace, but even in the developed nations women are still paid considerably less than men for the same work, millions of people are starving around the world and most of them are black, the wife of the first minister of Northern Ireland felt able to call homosexuality 'an abomination' in 2008, the Market, whether it is up or down, controls the lives of individuals, and vast corporations have consolidated their power over elected (and unelected) governments. In addition the planet is frying. Some fine souls

---

*In a British sitcom called *Till Death Us Do Part*, which portrayed a viciously racist, sexist working-class anti-hero as a lovable idiot, patronised by all around him.

are still battling; most of us who had the good fortune to be part of the Sixties are plain discouraged.

NOTES

Introduction

1 Rodrigo Fresàn, *Kensington Gardens*, translated by Natasha Wimmer, New York, Farrar Straus & Giroux, 2006.

Consuming the Sixties

2 Leviticus, 19:19.

Altering Realities

3 Timothy Leary, in Martin A. Lee and Bruce Shlain, *Acid Dreams: The Complete Social History of LSD: the CIA, the Sixties and Beyond* (New York, Grove Press, 1985), quoted in Jonathon Green, *All Dressed Up: The Sixties and the Counterculture*. London, Pimlico, 1999.

Body Work

4 Erica Jong, *Fear of Flying*, New York, Holt, Rinehart and Winston, 1973.

5 Jonathon Green (ed.), *Days in the Life: Voices from the English Underground 1961–1971*, London, Minerva, 1988.

6 Ibid.

7 Roy Jenkins, *Is Britain Civilised?*, 1959, quoted in Green, *All Dressed Up*.

Remaking the World

8 Tariq Ali, *Street Fighting Years*, London, Collins, 1987.

9 Ibid.

10 Henry James, *The Princess Casamassima*, London, Macmillan, 1886.

11 *Oz*, 32, quoted in Green, *All Dressed Up*.

12 The *Times* Leader article, written by William Rees-Mogg on 1 July 1967, quoted Alexander Pope in asking 'Who Breaks a Butterfly on a Wheel?' in response to the prison sentences handed out to Mick Jagger and Keith Richards for possession of drugs.

13 David Widgery, *Preserving Disorder*, London, Pluto Press, 1989.

14 Peter Buckman, *The Limits of Protest*, London, Gollancz, 1970, quoted in Green, *All Dressed Up*.

15 Widgery, *Preserving Disorder*, London, Pluto, 1989.

16 Ibid.

Projecting the Future

17 Leila Berg, *Risinghill: Death of a Comprehensive School*, London, Penguin Books, 1968.
18 Ivan Illich, *Deschooling Society*, New York, Harper & Row; London, Calder & Boyars, 1971.
19 Paul Goodman, John Holt, for example.
20 Illich, *Deschooling Society*.
21 Ibid.
22 Ibid.

Changing Our Minds

23 R. D. Laing, *The Divided Self*, (London, Tavistock, 1960), Penguin Books, 1965.
24 R. D. Laing, *The Politics of Experience and The Bird of Paradise*, London, Penguin Books.
25 Joseph Cambell, *The Hero with a Thousand Faces*, Princeton, Princeton University Press, 1949.
26 Mary Barnes, Joseph Burke, *Two Accounts of a Journey Through Madness* (1971), Free Association Books, 1991.
27 Ken Kesey, *One Flew Over the Cuckoo's Nest*, New York, Viking, 1962.
28 Thomas Szasz, *The Myth of Mental Illness*, New York, Harper & Row, 1961.
29 Green (ed.), *Days in the Life*.
30 Widgery, *Preserving Disorder*.